Printed Name of Signer		Signature
Address		

MW00902206

Date Notarized	Time	Am	Travel Fee
		Pm	

Service	Satisfactory Evidence of ID		ID Number
❑ Acknowledgment	❑ Driver's License	❑ ID Card	
			Date Issued
❑ Oath/Affirmation	❑ Credible Witness	❑ Passport	
			Expiration Date
❑ Jurat	❑ Known Personally		
			Issuer
❑ Other_____	❑ Other: _____		

Printed Name of Witness	Signature
Address	Phone No.
	Email
Notes/Comments	Record No.

Printed Name of Signer		Signature
Address		Phone No.
		Email

Date Notarized	Time	Am	Fee Charged	Travel Fee
		Pm		

Service	Satisfactory Evidence of ID		ID Number
❑ Acknowledgment	❑ Driver's License	❑ ID Card	
			Date Issued
❑ Oath/Affirmation	❑ Credible Witness	❑ Passport	
			Expiration Date
❑ Jurat	❑ Known Personally		
			Issuer
❑ Other_____	❑ Other: _____		

Printed Name of Witness	Signature
Address	Phone No.
	Email
Notes/Comments	Record No.

MW00902206

Printed Name of Signer		Signature	
Address		Phone No.	
		Email	

Date Notarized	Time	Am Pm	Fee Charged	Travel Fee

Service	Satisfactory Evidence of ID	ID Number
❏ Acknowledgment	❏ Driver's License ❏ ID Card	
		Date Issued
❏ Oath/Affirmation	❏ Credible Witness ❏ Passport	
		Expiration Date
❏ Jurat	❏ Known Personally	
❏ Other_____	❏ Other: _____	Issuer

Printed Name of Witness		Signature
Address		Phone No.
		Email
Notes/Comments		Record No.

Printed Name of Signer		Signature	
Address		Phone No.	
		Email	

Date Notarized	Time	Am Pm	Fee Charged	Travel Fee

Service	Satisfactory Evidence of ID	ID Number
❏ Acknowledgment	❏ Driver's License ❏ ID Card	
		Date Issued
❏ Oath/Affirmation	❏ Credible Witness ❏ Passport	
		Expiration Date
❏ Jurat	❏ Known Personally	
❏ Other_____	❏ Other: _____	Issuer

Printed Name of Witness		Signature
Address		Phone No.
		Email
Notes/Comments		Record No.

Printed Name of Signer			Signature	
Address			Phone No.	
			Email	
Date Notarized	Time	Am	Fee Charged	Travel Fee
		Pm		

Service	Satisfactory Evidence of ID		ID Number
❑ Acknowledgment	❑ Driver's License	❑ ID Card	
			Date Issued
❑ Oath/Affirmation	❑ Credible Witness	❑ Passport	Expiration Date
❑ Jurat	❑ Known Personally		Issuer
❑ Other_____	❑ Other: _____		

Printed Name of Witness	Signature
Address	Phone No.
	Email
Notes/Comments	Record No.

Printed Name of Signer			Signature	
Address			Phone No.	
			Email	
Date Notarized	Time	Am	Fee Charged	Travel Fee
		Pm		

Service	Satisfactory Evidence of ID		ID Number
❑ Acknowledgment	❑ Driver's License	❑ ID Card	
			Date Issued
❑ Oath/Affirmation	❑ Credible Witness	❑ Passport	Expiration Date
❑ Jurat	❑ Known Personally		Issuer
❑ Other_____	❑ Other: _____		

Printed Name of Witness	Signature
Address	Phone No.
	Email
Notes/Comments	Record No.

Printed Name of Signer		Signature	
Address		Phone No.	
		Email	

Date Notarized	Time	Am / Pm	Fee Charged	Travel Fee

Service	Satisfactory Evidence of ID	ID Number
❑ Acknowledgment	❑ Driver's License ❑ ID Card	
		Date Issued
❑ Oath/Affirmation	❑ Credible Witness ❑ Passport	
		Expiration Date
❑ Jurat	❑ Known Personally	
		Issuer
❑ Other_____	❑ Other: _____	

Printed Name of Witness		Signature
Address		Phone No.
		Email
Notes/Comments		Record No.

Printed Name of Signer		Signature	
Address		Phone No.	
		Email	

Date Notarized	Time	Am / Pm	Fee Charged	Travel Fee

Service	Satisfactory Evidence of ID	ID Number
❑ Acknowledgment	❑ Driver's License ❑ ID Card	
		Date Issued
❑ Oath/Affirmation	❑ Credible Witness ❑ Passport	
		Expiration Date
❑ Jurat	❑ Known Personally	
		Issuer
❑ Other_____	❑ Other: _____	

Printed Name of Witness		Signature
Address		Phone No.
		Email
Notes/Comments		Record No.

Printed Name of Signer		Signature	
Address		Phone No.	
		Email	

Date Notarized	Time	Am / Pm	Fee Charged	Travel Fee

Service
- ❑ Acknowledgment
- ❑ Oath/Affirmation
- ❑ Jurat
- ❑ Other_____

Satisfactory Evidence of ID
- ❑ Driver's License
- ❑ ID Card
- ❑ Credible Witness
- ❑ Passport
- ❑ Known Personally
- ❑ Other: _____

ID Number

Date Issued

Expiration Date

Issuer

Printed Name of Witness	Signature
Address	Phone No.
	Email
Notes/Comments	Record No.

Printed Name of Signer		Signature	
Address		Phone No.	
		Email	

Date Notarized	Time	Am / Pm	Fee Charged	Travel Fee

Service
- ❑ Acknowledgment
- ❑ Oath/Affirmation
- ❑ Jurat
- ❑ Other_____

Satisfactory Evidence of ID
- ❑ Driver's License
- ❑ ID Card
- ❑ Credible Witness
- ❑ Passport
- ❑ Known Personally
- ❑ Other: _____

ID Number

Date Issued

Expiration Date

Issuer

Printed Name of Witness	Signature
Address	Phone No.
	Email
Notes/Comments	Record No.

Printed Name of Signer		Signature	
Address		Phone No.	
		Email	

Date Notarized	Time	Am / Pm	Fee Charged	Travel Fee

Service	Satisfactory Evidence of ID	ID Number
❑ Acknowledgment	❑ Driver's License ❑ ID Card	
		Date Issued
❑ Oath/Affirmation	❑ Credible Witness ❑ Passport	
		Expiration Date
❑ Jurat	❑ Known Personally	
❑ Other_____	❑ Other: _____	Issuer

Printed Name of Witness		Signature
Address		Phone No.
		Email
Notes/Comments		Record No.

Printed Name of Signer		Signature	
Address		Phone No.	
		Email	

Date Notarized	Time	Am / Pm	Fee Charged	Travel Fee

Service	Satisfactory Evidence of ID	ID Number
❑ Acknowledgment	❑ Driver's License ❑ ID Card	
		Date Issued
❑ Oath/Affirmation	❑ Credible Witness ❑ Passport	
		Expiration Date
❑ Jurat	❑ Known Personally	
❑ Other_____	❑ Other: _____	Issuer

Printed Name of Witness		Signature
Address		Phone No.
		Email
Notes/Comments		Record No.

Printed Name of Signer			Signature	
Address			Phone No.	
			Email	

Date Notarized	Time	Am	Fee Charged	Travel Fee
		Pm		

Service	Satisfactory Evidence of ID		ID Number
❑ Acknowledgment	❑ Driver's License	❑ ID Card	
			Date Issued
❑ Oath/Affirmation	❑ Credible Witness	❑ Passport	
			Expiration Date
❑ Jurat	❑ Known Personally		
❑ Other_____	❑ Other: _____		Issuer

Printed Name of Witness	Signature
Address	Phone No.
	Email
Notes/Comments	Record No.

Printed Name of Signer			Signature	
Address			Phone No.	
			Email	

Date Notarized	Time	Am	Fee Charged	Travel Fee
		Pm		

Service	Satisfactory Evidence of ID		ID Number
❑ Acknowledgment	❑ Driver's License	❑ ID Card	
			Date Issued
❑ Oath/Affirmation	❑ Credible Witness	❑ Passport	
			Expiration Date
❑ Jurat	❑ Known Personally		
❑ Other_____	❑ Other: _____		Issuer

Printed Name of Witness	Signature
Address	Phone No.
	Email
Notes/Comments	Record No.

Printed Name of Signer		Signature	
Address		Phone No.	
		Email	

Date Notarized	Time	Am	Fee Charged	Travel Fee
		Pm		

Service	Satisfactory Evidence of ID		ID Number
❑ Acknowledgment	❑ Driver's License	❑ ID Card	
			Date Issued
❑ Oath/Affirmation	❑ Credible Witness	❑ Passport	
			Expiration Date
❑ Jurat	❑ Known Personally		
			Issuer
❑ Other_____	❑ Other: _____		

Printed Name of Witness	Signature
Address	Phone No.
	Email
Notes/Comments	Record No.

Printed Name of Signer		Signature	
Address		Phone No.	
		Email	

Date Notarized	Time	Am	Fee Charged	Travel Fee
		Pm		

Service	Satisfactory Evidence of ID		ID Number
❑ Acknowledgment	❑ Driver's License	❑ ID Card	
			Date Issued
❑ Oath/Affirmation	❑ Credible Witness	❑ Passport	
			Expiration Date
❑ Jurat	❑ Known Personally		
			Issuer
❑ Other_____	❑ Other: _____		

Printed Name of Witness	Signature
Address	Phone No.
	Email
Notes/Comments	Record No.

Printed Name of Signer				Signature	
Address			Phone No.		
			Email		
Date Notarized	Time	Am / Pm	Fee Charged		Travel Fee

Service	Satisfactory Evidence of ID		ID Number
❑ Acknowledgment	❑ Driver's License	❑ ID Card	Date Issued
❑ Oath/Affirmation	❑ Credible Witness	❑ Passport	Expiration Date
❑ Jurat	❑ Known Personally		Issuer
❑ Other_____	❑ Other: _____		

Printed Name of Witness		Signature
Address		Phone No.
		Email
Notes/Comments		Record No.

Printed Name of Signer				Signature	
Address			Phone No.		
			Email		
Date Notarized	Time	Am / Pm	Fee Charged		Travel Fee

Service	Satisfactory Evidence of ID		ID Number
❑ Acknowledgment	❑ Driver's License	❑ ID Card	Date Issued
❑ Oath/Affirmation	❑ Credible Witness	❑ Passport	Expiration Date
❑ Jurat	❑ Known Personally		Issuer
❑ Other_____	❑ Other: _____		

Printed Name of Witness		Signature
Address		Phone No.
		Email
Notes/Comments		Record No.

Printed Name of Signer		Signature	

Address	Phone No.	
	Email	

Date Notarized	Time	Am / Pm	Fee Charged	Travel Fee

Service	Satisfactory Evidence of ID		ID Number
☐ Acknowledgment	☐ Driver's License	☐ ID Card	
			Date Issued
☐ Oath/Affirmation	☐ Credible Witness	☐ Passport	
			Expiration Date
☐ Jurat	☐ Known Personally		
			Issuer
☐ Other_____	☐ Other: _____		

Printed Name of Witness	Signature

Address	Phone No.
	Email

Notes/Comments	Record No.

Printed Name of Signer		Signature	

Address	Phone No.	
	Email	

Date Notarized	Time	Am / Pm	Fee Charged	Travel Fee

Service	Satisfactory Evidence of ID		ID Number
☐ Acknowledgment	☐ Driver's License	☐ ID Card	
			Date Issued
☐ Oath/Affirmation	☐ Credible Witness	☐ Passport	
			Expiration Date
☐ Jurat	☐ Known Personally		
			Issuer
☐ Other_____	☐ Other: _____		

Printed Name of Witness	Signature

Address	Phone No.
	Email

Notes/Comments	Record No.

Printed Name of Signer		Signature	
Address		Phone No.	
		Email	

Date Notarized	Time	Am	Fee Charged	Travel Fee
		Pm		

Service	Satisfactory Evidence of ID		ID Number
❑ Acknowledgment	❑ Driver's License	❑ ID Card	
			Date Issued
❑ Oath/Affirmation	❑ Credible Witness	❑ Passport	
			Expiration Date
❑ Jurat	❑ Known Personally		
❑ Other_____	❑ Other: _____		Issuer

Printed Name of Witness	Signature
Address	Phone No.
	Email
Notes/Comments	Record No.

Printed Name of Signer		Signature	
Address		Phone No.	
		Email	

Date Notarized	Time	Am	Fee Charged	Travel Fee
		Pm		

Service	Satisfactory Evidence of ID		ID Number
❑ Acknowledgment	❑ Driver's License	❑ ID Card	
			Date Issued
❑ Oath/Affirmation	❑ Credible Witness	❑ Passport	
			Expiration Date
❑ Jurat	❑ Known Personally		
❑ Other_____	❑ Other: _____		Issuer

Printed Name of Witness	Signature
Address	Phone No.
	Email
Notes/Comments	Record No.

Printed Name of Signer		Signature	
Address		Phone No.	
		Email	

Date Notarized	Time	Am Pm	Fee Charged	Travel Fee

Service	Satisfactory Evidence of ID	ID Number
❑ Acknowledgment	❑ Driver's License ❑ ID Card	Date Issued
❑ Oath/Affirmation	❑ Credible Witness ❑ Passport	Expiration Date
❑ Jurat	❑ Known Personally	Issuer
❑ Other_____	❑ Other: _____	

Printed Name of Witness		Signature
Address		Phone No.
		Email
Notes/Comments		Record No.

Printed Name of Signer		Signature	
Address		Phone No.	
		Email	

Date Notarized	Time	Am Pm	Fee Charged	Travel Fee

Service	Satisfactory Evidence of ID	ID Number
❑ Acknowledgment	❑ Driver's License ❑ ID Card	Date Issued
❑ Oath/Affirmation	❑ Credible Witness ❑ Passport	Expiration Date
❑ Jurat	❑ Known Personally	Issuer
❑ Other_____	❑ Other: _____	

Printed Name of Witness		Signature
Address		Phone No.
		Email
Notes/Comments		Record No.

Printed Name of Signer			Signature	
Address			Phone No.	
			Email	

Date Notarized	Time	Am Pm	Fee Charged	Travel Fee

Service	Satisfactory Evidence of ID		ID Number
❑ Acknowledgment	❑ Driver's License	❑ ID Card	Date Issued
❑ Oath/Affirmation	❑ Credible Witness	❑ Passport	Expiration Date
❑ Jurat	❑ Known Personally		Issuer
❑ Other_____	❑ Other: _____		

Printed Name of Witness	Signature
Address	Phone No.
	Email
Notes/Comments	**Record No.**

Printed Name of Signer			Signature	
Address			Phone No.	
			Email	

Date Notarized	Time	Am Pm	Fee Charged	Travel Fee

Service	Satisfactory Evidence of ID		ID Number
❑ Acknowledgment	❑ Driver's License	❑ ID Card	Date Issued
❑ Oath/Affirmation	❑ Credible Witness	❑ Passport	Expiration Date
❑ Jurat	❑ Known Personally		Issuer
❑ Other_____	❑ Other: _____		

Printed Name of Witness	Signature
Address	Phone No.
	Email
Notes/Comments	**Record No.**

Printed Name of Signer			Signature	
Address		Phone No.		
		Email		

Date Notarized	Time	Am Pm	Fee Charged	Travel Fee

Service	Satisfactory Evidence of ID	ID Number
❑ Acknowledgment	❑ Driver's License ❑ ID Card	
		Date Issued
❑ Oath/Affirmation	❑ Credible Witness ❑ Passport	
		Expiration Date
❑ Jurat	❑ Known Personally	
❑ Other_____	❑ Other: _____	Issuer

Printed Name of Witness		Signature
Address		Phone No.
		Email
Notes/Comments		Record No.

Printed Name of Signer			Signature	
Address		Phone No.		
		Email		

Date Notarized	Time	Am Pm	Fee Charged	Travel Fee

Service	Satisfactory Evidence of ID	ID Number
❑ Acknowledgment	❑ Driver's License ❑ ID Card	
		Date Issued
❑ Oath/Affirmation	❑ Credible Witness ❑ Passport	
		Expiration Date
❑ Jurat	❑ Known Personally	
❑ Other_____	❑ Other: _____	Issuer

Printed Name of Witness		Signature
Address		Phone No.
		Email
Notes/Comments		Record No.

Printed Name of Signer		Signature	
Address		Phone No.	
		Email	

Date Notarized	Time	Am	Fee Charged	Travel Fee
		Pm		

Service	Satisfactory Evidence of ID		ID Number
❑ Acknowledgment	❑ Driver's License	❑ ID Card	Date Issued
❑ Oath/Affirmation	❑ Credible Witness	❑ Passport	Expiration Date
❑ Jurat	❑ Known Personally		Issuer
❑ Other_____	❑ Other: _____		

Printed Name of Witness		Signature
Address		Phone No.
		Email
Notes/Comments		Record No.

Printed Name of Signer		Signature	
Address		Phone No.	
		Email	

Date Notarized	Time	Am	Fee Charged	Travel Fee
		Pm		

Service	Satisfactory Evidence of ID		ID Number
❑ Acknowledgment	❑ Driver's License	❑ ID Card	Date Issued
❑ Oath/Affirmation	❑ Credible Witness	❑ Passport	Expiration Date
❑ Jurat	❑ Known Personally		Issuer
❑ Other_____	❑ Other: _____		

Printed Name of Witness		Signature
Address		Phone No.
		Email
Notes/Comments		Record No.

Printed Name of Signer		Signature	

Address		Phone No.	
		Email	

Date Notarized	Time	Am	Fee Charged	Travel Fee
		Pm		

Service	Satisfactory Evidence of ID		ID Number
❑ Acknowledgment	❑ Driver's License	❑ ID Card	Date Issued
❑ Oath/Affirmation	❑ Credible Witness	❑ Passport	Expiration Date
❑ Jurat	❑ Known Personally		Issuer
❑ Other_____	❑ Other: _____		

Printed Name of Witness	Signature
Address	Phone No.
	Email
Notes/Comments	Record No.

Printed Name of Signer		Signature	

Address		Phone No.	
		Email	

Date Notarized	Time	Am	Fee Charged	Travel Fee
		Pm		

Service	Satisfactory Evidence of ID		ID Number
❑ Acknowledgment	❑ Driver's License	❑ ID Card	Date Issued
❑ Oath/Affirmation	❑ Credible Witness	❑ Passport	Expiration Date
❑ Jurat	❑ Known Personally		Issuer
❑ Other_____	❑ Other: _____		

Printed Name of Witness	Signature
Address	Phone No.
	Email
Notes/Comments	Record No.

Printed Name of Signer			Signature	
Address			Phone No.	
			Email	
Date Notarized	Time	Am / Pm	Fee Charged	Travel Fee

Service	Satisfactory Evidence of ID		ID Number
❑ Acknowledgment	❑ Driver's License	❑ ID Card	
			Date Issued
❑ Oath/Affirmation	❑ Credible Witness	❑ Passport	
			Expiration Date
❑ Jurat	❑ Known Personally		
❑ Other_____	❑ Other: _____		Issuer

Printed Name of Witness		Signature	
Address		Phone No.	
		Email	
Notes/Comments		Record No.	

Printed Name of Signer			Signature	
Address			Phone No.	
			Email	
Date Notarized	Time	Am / Pm	Fee Charged	Travel Fee

Service	Satisfactory Evidence of ID		ID Number
❑ Acknowledgment	❑ Driver's License	❑ ID Card	
			Date Issued
❑ Oath/Affirmation	❑ Credible Witness	❑ Passport	
			Expiration Date
❑ Jurat	❑ Known Personally		
❑ Other_____	❑ Other: _____		Issuer

Printed Name of Witness		Signature	
Address		Phone No.	
		Email	
Notes/Comments		Record No.	

Printed Name of Signer		Signature	
Address		Phone No.	
		Email	

Date Notarized	Time	Am Pm	Fee Charged	Travel Fee

Service	Satisfactory Evidence of ID	ID Number
❑ Acknowledgment	❑ Driver's License ❑ ID Card	
		Date Issued
❑ Oath/Affirmation	❑ Credible Witness ❑ Passport	
		Expiration Date
❑ Jurat	❑ Known Personally	
❑ Other_____	❑ Other: _____	Issuer

Printed Name of Witness		Signature
Address		Phone No.
		Email
Notes/Comments		Record No.

Printed Name of Signer		Signature	
Address		Phone No.	
		Email	

Date Notarized	Time	Am Pm	Fee Charged	Travel Fee

Service	Satisfactory Evidence of ID	ID Number
❑ Acknowledgment	❑ Driver's License ❑ ID Card	
		Date Issued
❑ Oath/Affirmation	❑ Credible Witness ❑ Passport	
		Expiration Date
❑ Jurat	❑ Known Personally	
❑ Other_____	❑ Other: _____	Issuer

Printed Name of Witness		Signature
Address		Phone No.
		Email
Notes/Comments		Record No.

Printed Name of Signer		Signature	
Address		Phone No.	
		Email	

Date Notarized		Time	Am Pm	Fee Charged	Travel Fee

Service	Satisfactory Evidence of ID		ID Number
❏ Acknowledgment	❏ Driver's License	❏ ID Card	
			Date Issued
❏ Oath/Affirmation	❏ Credible Witness	❏ Passport	
			Expiration Date
❏ Jurat	❏ Known Personally		
❏ Other_____	❏ Other: _____		Issuer

Printed Name of Witness	Signature
Address	Phone No.
	Email
Notes/Comments	Record No.

Printed Name of Signer		Signature	
Address		Phone No.	
		Email	

Date Notarized		Time	Am Pm	Fee Charged	Travel Fee

Service	Satisfactory Evidence of ID		ID Number
❏ Acknowledgment	❏ Driver's License	❏ ID Card	
			Date Issued
❏ Oath/Affirmation	❏ Credible Witness	❏ Passport	
			Expiration Date
❏ Jurat	❏ Known Personally		
❏ Other_____	❏ Other: _____		Issuer

Printed Name of Witness	Signature
Address	Phone No.
	Email
Notes/Comments	Record No.

Printed Name of Signer		Signature	

Address		Phone No.	
		Email	

Date Notarized	Time	Am	Fee Charged	Travel Fee
		Pm		

Service	Satisfactory Evidence of ID		ID Number
❑ Acknowledgment	❑ Driver's License	❑ ID Card	
			Date Issued
❑ Oath/Affirmation	❑ Credible Witness	❑ Passport	
			Expiration Date
❑ Jurat	❑ Known Personally		
			Issuer
❑ Other_____	❑ Other: _____		

Printed Name of Witness		Signature	

Address		Phone No.	
		Email	

Notes/Comments		Record No.	

Printed Name of Signer		Signature	

Address		Phone No.	
		Email	

Date Notarized	Time	Am	Fee Charged	Travel Fee
		Pm		

Service	Satisfactory Evidence of ID		ID Number
❑ Acknowledgment	❑ Driver's License	❑ ID Card	
			Date Issued
❑ Oath/Affirmation	❑ Credible Witness	❑ Passport	
			Expiration Date
❑ Jurat	❑ Known Personally		
			Issuer
❑ Other_____	❑ Other: _____		

Printed Name of Witness		Signature	

Address		Phone No.	
		Email	

Notes/Comments		Record No.	

Printed Name of Signer		Signature	
Address		Phone No.	
		Email	

Date Notarized	Time	Am	Fee Charged	Travel Fee
		Pm		

Service	Satisfactory Evidence of ID		ID Number
❑ Acknowledgment	❑ Driver's License	❑ ID Card	
			Date Issued
❑ Oath/Affirmation	❑ Credible Witness	❑ Passport	Expiration Date
❑ Jurat	❑ Known Personally		Issuer
❑ Other_____	❑ Other: _____		

Printed Name of Witness	Signature
Address	Phone No.
	Email
Notes/Comments	Record No.

Printed Name of Signer		Signature	
Address		Phone No.	
		Email	

Date Notarized	Time	Am	Fee Charged	Travel Fee
		Pm		

Service	Satisfactory Evidence of ID		ID Number
❑ Acknowledgment	❑ Driver's License	❑ ID Card	
			Date Issued
❑ Oath/Affirmation	❑ Credible Witness	❑ Passport	Expiration Date
❑ Jurat	❑ Known Personally		Issuer
❑ Other_____	❑ Other: _____		

Printed Name of Witness	Signature
Address	Phone No.
	Email
Notes/Comments	Record No.

Printed Name of Signer				Signature	
Address			**Phone No.**		
			Email		

Date Notarized	Time	Am		Fee Charged	Travel Fee
		Pm			

Service	Satisfactory Evidence of ID		ID Number
❑ Acknowledgment	❑ Driver's License	❑ ID Card	
			Date Issued
❑ Oath/Affirmation	❑ Credible Witness	❑ Passport	
			Expiration Date
❑ Jurat	❑ Known Personally		
			Issuer
❑ Other_____	❑ Other: _____		

Printed Name of Witness	Signature
Address	**Phone No.**
	Email
Notes/Comments	**Record No.**

Printed Name of Signer				Signature	
Address			**Phone No.**		
			Email		

Date Notarized	Time	Am		Fee Charged	Travel Fee
		Pm			

Service	Satisfactory Evidence of ID		ID Number
❑ Acknowledgment	❑ Driver's License	❑ ID Card	
			Date Issued
❑ Oath/Affirmation	❑ Credible Witness	❑ Passport	
			Expiration Date
❑ Jurat	❑ Known Personally		
			Issuer
❑ Other_____	❑ Other: _____		

Printed Name of Witness	Signature
Address	**Phone No.**
	Email
Notes/Comments	**Record No.**

Printed Name of Signer		Signature	
Address		Phone No.	
		Email	

Date Notarized	Time	Am Pm	Fee Charged	Travel Fee

Service	Satisfactory Evidence of ID		ID Number
❑ Acknowledgment	❑ Driver's License	❑ ID Card	
			Date Issued
❑ Oath/Affirmation	❑ Credible Witness	❑ Passport	
			Expiration Date
❑ Jurat	❑ Known Personally		
			Issuer
❑ Other_____	❑ Other: _____		

Printed Name of Witness		Signature	
Address		Phone No.	
		Email	
Notes/Comments		Record No.	

Printed Name of Signer		Signature	
Address		Phone No.	
		Email	

Date Notarized	Time	Am Pm	Fee Charged	Travel Fee

Service	Satisfactory Evidence of ID		ID Number
❑ Acknowledgment	❑ Driver's License	❑ ID Card	
			Date Issued
❑ Oath/Affirmation	❑ Credible Witness	❑ Passport	
			Expiration Date
❑ Jurat	❑ Known Personally		
			Issuer
❑ Other_____	❑ Other: _____		

Printed Name of Witness		Signature	
Address		Phone No.	
		Email	
Notes/Comments		Record No.	

Printed Name of Signer		Signature	

Address		Phone No.	
		Email	

Date Notarized	Time	Am		Fee Charged	Travel Fee
		Pm			

Service	Satisfactory Evidence of ID		ID Number
❑ Acknowledgment	❑ Driver's License	❑ ID Card	Date Issued
❑ Oath/Affirmation	❑ Credible Witness	❑ Passport	Expiration Date
❑ Jurat	❑ Known Personally		Issuer
❑ Other_____	❑ Other: _____		

Printed Name of Witness	Signature

Address	Phone No.
	Email

Notes/Comments	Record No.

Printed Name of Signer		Signature	

Address		Phone No.	
		Email	

Date Notarized	Time	Am		Fee Charged	Travel Fee
		Pm			

Service	Satisfactory Evidence of ID		ID Number
❑ Acknowledgment	❑ Driver's License	❑ ID Card	Date Issued
❑ Oath/Affirmation	❑ Credible Witness	❑ Passport	Expiration Date
❑ Jurat	❑ Known Personally		Issuer
❑ Other_____	❑ Other: _____		

Printed Name of Witness	Signature

Address	Phone No.
	Email

Notes/Comments	Record No.

Printed Name of Signer			Signature	
Address			Phone No.	
			Email	

Date Notarized	Time	Am	Fee Charged	Travel Fee
		Pm		

Service	Satisfactory Evidence of ID		ID Number
❑ Acknowledgment	❑ Driver's License	❑ ID Card	
			Date Issued
❑ Oath/Affirmation	❑ Credible Witness	❑ Passport	
			Expiration Date
❑ Jurat	❑ Known Personally		
			Issuer
❑ Other_____	❑ Other: _____		

Printed Name of Witness	Signature
Address	Phone No.
	Email
Notes/Comments	Record No.

Printed Name of Signer			Signature	
Address			Phone No.	
			Email	

Date Notarized	Time	Am	Fee Charged	Travel Fee
		Pm		

Service	Satisfactory Evidence of ID		ID Number
❑ Acknowledgment	❑ Driver's License	❑ ID Card	
			Date Issued
❑ Oath/Affirmation	❑ Credible Witness	❑ Passport	
			Expiration Date
❑ Jurat	❑ Known Personally		
			Issuer
❑ Other_____	❑ Other: _____		

Printed Name of Witness	Signature
Address	Phone No.
	Email
Notes/Comments	Record No.

Printed Name of Signer				Signature		
Address			**Phone No.**			
			Email			
Date Notarized	**Time**	**Am** **Pm**		**Fee Charged**		**Travel Fee**

Service	Satisfactory Evidence of ID		ID Number
❑ Acknowledgment	❑ Driver's License	❑ ID Card	Date Issued
❑ Oath/Affirmation	❑ Credible Witness	❑ Passport	Expiration Date
❑ Jurat	❑ Known Personally		Issuer
❑ Other_____	❑ Other: _____		

Printed Name of Witness	Signature
Address	**Phone No.**
	Email
Notes/Comments	**Record No.**

Printed Name of Signer				Signature		
Address			**Phone No.**			
			Email			
Date Notarized	**Time**	**Am** **Pm**		**Fee Charged**		**Travel Fee**

Service	Satisfactory Evidence of ID		ID Number
❑ Acknowledgment	❑ Driver's License	❑ ID Card	Date Issued
❑ Oath/Affirmation	❑ Credible Witness	❑ Passport	Expiration Date
❑ Jurat	❑ Known Personally		Issuer
❑ Other_____	❑ Other: _____		

Printed Name of Witness	Signature
Address	**Phone No.**
	Email
Notes/Comments	**Record No.**

Printed Name of Signer		Signature	
Address		Phone No.	
		Email	

Date Notarized	Time	Am / Pm	Fee Charged	Travel Fee

Service	Satisfactory Evidence of ID		ID Number
❑ Acknowledgment	❑ Driver's License	❑ ID Card	Date Issued
❑ Oath/Affirmation	❑ Credible Witness	❑ Passport	Expiration Date
❑ Jurat	❑ Known Personally		Issuer
❑ Other_____	❑ Other: _____		

Printed Name of Witness	Signature
Address	Phone No.
	Email
Notes/Comments	Record No.

Printed Name of Signer		Signature	
Address		Phone No.	
		Email	

Date Notarized	Time	Am / Pm	Fee Charged	Travel Fee

Service	Satisfactory Evidence of ID		ID Number
❑ Acknowledgment	❑ Driver's License	❑ ID Card	Date Issued
❑ Oath/Affirmation	❑ Credible Witness	❑ Passport	Expiration Date
❑ Jurat	❑ Known Personally		Issuer
❑ Other_____	❑ Other: _____		

Printed Name of Witness	Signature
Address	Phone No.
	Email
Notes/Comments	Record No.

Printed Name of Signer		Signature	

Address		Phone No.	
		Email	

Date Notarized	Time	Am	Fee Charged	Travel Fee
		Pm		

Service	Satisfactory Evidence of ID		ID Number
❑ Acknowledgment	❑ Driver's License	❑ ID Card	Date Issued
❑ Oath/Affirmation	❑ Credible Witness	❑ Passport	Expiration Date
❑ Jurat	❑ Known Personally		Issuer
❑ Other_____	❑ Other: _____		

Printed Name of Witness	Signature
Address	Phone No.
	Email
Notes/Comments	Record No.

Printed Name of Signer		Signature	

Address		Phone No.	
		Email	

Date Notarized	Time	Am	Fee Charged	Travel Fee
		Pm		

Service	Satisfactory Evidence of ID		ID Number
❑ Acknowledgment	❑ Driver's License	❑ ID Card	Date Issued
❑ Oath/Affirmation	❑ Credible Witness	❑ Passport	Expiration Date
❑ Jurat	❑ Known Personally		Issuer
❑ Other_____	❑ Other: _____		

Printed Name of Witness	Signature
Address	Phone No.
	Email
Notes/Comments	Record No.

Printed Name of Signer		Signature	

Address	Phone No.	
	Email	

Date Notarized	Time	Am	Fee Charged	Travel Fee
		Pm		

Service	Satisfactory Evidence of ID		ID Number
❑ Acknowledgment	❑ Driver's License	❑ ID Card	
			Date Issued
❑ Oath/Affirmation	❑ Credible Witness	❑ Passport	Expiration Date
❑ Jurat	❑ Known Personally		Issuer
❑ Other_____	❑ Other: _____		

Printed Name of Witness	Signature	
Address	Phone No.	
	Email	
Notes/Comments	Record No.	

Printed Name of Signer		Signature	

Address	Phone No.	
	Email	

Date Notarized	Time	Am	Fee Charged	Travel Fee
		Pm		

Service	Satisfactory Evidence of ID		ID Number
❑ Acknowledgment	❑ Driver's License	❑ ID Card	
			Date Issued
❑ Oath/Affirmation	❑ Credible Witness	❑ Passport	Expiration Date
❑ Jurat	❑ Known Personally		Issuer
❑ Other_____	❑ Other: _____		

Printed Name of Witness	Signature	
Address	Phone No.	
	Email	
Notes/Comments	Record No.	

Printed Name of Signer		Signature	

Address		Phone No.	
		Email	

Date Notarized	Time	Am	Fee Charged	Travel Fee
		Pm		

Service	Satisfactory Evidence of ID		ID Number
❑ Acknowledgment	❑ Driver's License	❑ ID Card	
			Date Issued
❑ Oath/Affirmation	❑ Credible Witness	❑ Passport	
			Expiration Date
❑ Jurat	❑ Known Personally		
			Issuer
❑ Other_____	❑ Other: _____		

Printed Name of Witness	Signature

Address	Phone No.
	Email

Notes/Comments	Record No.

Printed Name of Signer		Signature	

Address		Phone No.	
		Email	

Date Notarized	Time	Am	Fee Charged	Travel Fee
		Pm		

Service	Satisfactory Evidence of ID		ID Number
❑ Acknowledgment	❑ Driver's License	❑ ID Card	
			Date Issued
❑ Oath/Affirmation	❑ Credible Witness	❑ Passport	
			Expiration Date
❑ Jurat	❑ Known Personally		
			Issuer
❑ Other_____	❑ Other: _____		

Printed Name of Witness	Signature

Address	Phone No.
	Email

Notes/Comments	Record No.

Printed Name of Signer		Signature	
Address		Phone No.	
		Email	

Date Notarized	Time	Am / Pm	Fee Charged	Travel Fee

Service	Satisfactory Evidence of ID		ID Number
❑ Acknowledgment	❑ Driver's License	❑ ID Card	
			Date Issued
❑ Oath/Affirmation	❑ Credible Witness	❑ Passport	
			Expiration Date
❑ Jurat	❑ Known Personally		
			Issuer
❑ Other_____	❑ Other: _____		

Printed Name of Witness	Signature
Address	Phone No.
	Email
Notes/Comments	Record No.

Printed Name of Signer		Signature	
Address		Phone No.	
		Email	

Date Notarized	Time	Am / Pm	Fee Charged	Travel Fee

Service	Satisfactory Evidence of ID		ID Number
❑ Acknowledgment	❑ Driver's License	❑ ID Card	
			Date Issued
❑ Oath/Affirmation	❑ Credible Witness	❑ Passport	
			Expiration Date
❑ Jurat	❑ Known Personally		
			Issuer
❑ Other_____	❑ Other: _____		

Printed Name of Witness	Signature
Address	Phone No.
	Email
Notes/Comments	Record No.

Printed Name of Signer		Signature	

Address		Phone No.	
		Email	

Date Notarized	Time	Am	Fee Charged	Travel Fee
		Pm		

Service	Satisfactory Evidence of ID	ID Number
❑ Acknowledgment	❑ Driver's License ❑ ID Card	
		Date Issued
❑ Oath/Affirmation	❑ Credible Witness ❑ Passport	
		Expiration Date
❑ Jurat	❑ Known Personally	
		Issuer
❑ Other_____	❑ Other: _____	

Printed Name of Witness	Signature
Address	Phone No.
	Email
Notes/Comments	Record No.

Printed Name of Signer		Signature	

Address		Phone No.	
		Email	

Date Notarized	Time	Am	Fee Charged	Travel Fee
		Pm		

Service	Satisfactory Evidence of ID	ID Number
❑ Acknowledgment	❑ Driver's License ❑ ID Card	
		Date Issued
❑ Oath/Affirmation	❑ Credible Witness ❑ Passport	
		Expiration Date
❑ Jurat	❑ Known Personally	
		Issuer
❑ Other_____	❑ Other: _____	

Printed Name of Witness	Signature
Address	Phone No.
	Email
Notes/Comments	Record No.

Printed Name of Signer				Signature	
Address			Phone No.		
			Email		
Date Notarized	Time	Am	Fee Charged		Travel Fee
		Pm			

Service	Satisfactory Evidence of ID		ID Number
❏ Acknowledgment	❏ Driver's License	❏ ID Card	
			Date Issued
❏ Oath/Affirmation	❏ Credible Witness	❏ Passport	
			Expiration Date
❏ Jurat	❏ Known Personally		
			Issuer
❏ Other_____	❏ Other: _____		

Printed Name of Witness	Signature
Address	Phone No.
	Email
Notes/Comments	Record No.

Printed Name of Signer				Signature	
Address			Phone No.		
			Email		
Date Notarized	Time	Am	Fee Charged		Travel Fee
		Pm			

Service	Satisfactory Evidence of ID		ID Number
❏ Acknowledgment	❏ Driver's License	❏ ID Card	
			Date Issued
❏ Oath/Affirmation	❏ Credible Witness	❏ Passport	
			Expiration Date
❏ Jurat	❏ Known Personally		
			Issuer
❏ Other_____	❏ Other: _____		

Printed Name of Witness	Signature
Address	Phone No.
	Email
Notes/Comments	Record No.

Printed Name of Signer		Signature	
Address		**Phone No.**	
		Email	

Date Notarized	Time	Am	Fee Charged	Travel Fee
		Pm		

Service	Satisfactory Evidence of ID		ID Number
❑ Acknowledgment	❑ Driver's License	❑ ID Card	
			Date Issued
❑ Oath/Affirmation	❑ Credible Witness	❑ Passport	Expiration Date
❑ Jurat	❑ Known Personally		Issuer
❑ Other_____	❑ Other: _____		

Printed Name of Witness		Signature	
Address		**Phone No.**	
		Email	
Notes/Comments		**Record No.**	

Printed Name of Signer		Signature	
Address		**Phone No.**	
		Email	

Date Notarized	Time	Am	Fee Charged	Travel Fee
		Pm		

Service	Satisfactory Evidence of ID		ID Number
❑ Acknowledgment	❑ Driver's License	❑ ID Card	
			Date Issued
❑ Oath/Affirmation	❑ Credible Witness	❑ Passport	Expiration Date
❑ Jurat	❑ Known Personally		Issuer
❑ Other_____	❑ Other: _____		

Printed Name of Witness		Signature	
Address		**Phone No.**	
		Email	
Notes/Comments		**Record No.**	

Printed Name of Signer		Signature	
Address		Phone No.	
		Email	

Date Notarized	Time	Am	Fee Charged	Travel Fee
		Pm		

Service	Satisfactory Evidence of ID		ID Number
❑ Acknowledgment	❑ Driver's License	❑ ID Card	
			Date Issued
❑ Oath/Affirmation	❑ Credible Witness	❑ Passport	
			Expiration Date
❑ Jurat	❑ Known Personally		
			Issuer
❑ Other_____	❑ Other: _____		

Printed Name of Witness		Signature
Address		Phone No.
		Email
Notes/Comments		Record No.

Printed Name of Signer		Signature	
Address		Phone No.	
		Email	

Date Notarized	Time	Am	Fee Charged	Travel Fee
		Pm		

Service	Satisfactory Evidence of ID		ID Number
❑ Acknowledgment	❑ Driver's License	❑ ID Card	
			Date Issued
❑ Oath/Affirmation	❑ Credible Witness	❑ Passport	
			Expiration Date
❑ Jurat	❑ Known Personally		
			Issuer
❑ Other_____	❑ Other: _____		

Printed Name of Witness		Signature
Address		Phone No.
		Email
Notes/Comments		Record No.

Printed Name of Signer				Signature	
Address			Phone No.		
			Email		
Date Notarized	Time	Am		Fee Charged	Travel Fee
		Pm			

Service	Satisfactory Evidence of ID		ID Number
❑ Acknowledgment	❑ Driver's License	❑ ID Card	
			Date Issued
❑ Oath/Affirmation	❑ Credible Witness	❑ Passport	
			Expiration Date
❑ Jurat	❑ Known Personally		
❑ Other_____	❑ Other: _____		Issuer

Printed Name of Witness	Signature
Address	Phone No.
	Email
Notes/Comments	Record No.

Printed Name of Signer				Signature	
Address			Phone No.		
			Email		
Date Notarized	Time	Am		Fee Charged	Travel Fee
		Pm			

Service	Satisfactory Evidence of ID		ID Number
❑ Acknowledgment	❑ Driver's License	❑ ID Card	
			Date Issued
❑ Oath/Affirmation	❑ Credible Witness	❑ Passport	
			Expiration Date
❑ Jurat	❑ Known Personally		
❑ Other_____	❑ Other: _____		Issuer

Printed Name of Witness	Signature
Address	Phone No.
	Email
Notes/Comments	Record No.

Printed Name of Signer			Signature	
Address			Phone No.	
			Email	

Date Notarized	Time	Am	Fee Charged	Travel Fee
		Pm		

Service	Satisfactory Evidence of ID		ID Number
❑ Acknowledgment	❑ Driver's License	❑ ID Card	
			Date Issued
❑ Oath/Affirmation	❑ Credible Witness	❑ Passport	
			Expiration Date
❑ Jurat	❑ Known Personally		
			Issuer
❑ Other_____	❑ Other: _____		

Printed Name of Witness	Signature
Address	Phone No.
	Email
Notes/Comments	Record No.

Printed Name of Signer			Signature	
Address			Phone No.	
			Email	

Date Notarized	Time	Am	Fee Charged	Travel Fee
		Pm		

Service	Satisfactory Evidence of ID		ID Number
❑ Acknowledgment	❑ Driver's License	❑ ID Card	
			Date Issued
❑ Oath/Affirmation	❑ Credible Witness	❑ Passport	
			Expiration Date
❑ Jurat	❑ Known Personally		
			Issuer
❑ Other_____	❑ Other: _____		

Printed Name of Witness	Signature
Address	Phone No.
	Email
Notes/Comments	Record No.

Printed Name of Signer		Signature	

Address		Phone No.	
		Email	

Date Notarized	Time	Am Pm	Fee Charged	Travel Fee

Service	Satisfactory Evidence of ID	ID Number
❑ Acknowledgment	❑ Driver's License ❑ ID Card	
		Date Issued
❑ Oath/Affirmation	❑ Credible Witness ❑ Passport	
		Expiration Date
❑ Jurat	❑ Known Personally	
		Issuer
❑ Other_____	❑ Other: _____	

Printed Name of Witness		Signature	

Address		Phone No.	
		Email	

Notes/Comments		Record No.	

Printed Name of Signer		Signature	

Address		Phone No.	
		Email	

Date Notarized	Time	Am Pm	Fee Charged	Travel Fee

Service	Satisfactory Evidence of ID	ID Number
❑ Acknowledgment	❑ Driver's License ❑ ID Card	
		Date Issued
❑ Oath/Affirmation	❑ Credible Witness ❑ Passport	
		Expiration Date
❑ Jurat	❑ Known Personally	
		Issuer
❑ Other_____	❑ Other: _____	

Printed Name of Witness		Signature	

Address		Phone No.	
		Email	

Notes/Comments		Record No.	

Printed Name of Signer				Signature	
Address			Phone No.		
			Email		

Date Notarized	Time	Am	Fee Charged	Travel Fee
		Pm		

Service	Satisfactory Evidence of ID		ID Number
❑ Acknowledgment	❑ Driver's License	❑ ID Card	
			Date Issued
❑ Oath/Affirmation	❑ Credible Witness	❑ Passport	
			Expiration Date
❑ Jurat	❑ Known Personally		
			Issuer
❑ Other_____	❑ Other: _____		

Printed Name of Witness	Signature
Address	Phone No.
	Email
Notes/Comments	Record No.

Printed Name of Signer				Signature	
Address			Phone No.		
			Email		

Date Notarized	Time	Am	Fee Charged	Travel Fee
		Pm		

Service	Satisfactory Evidence of ID		ID Number
❑ Acknowledgment	❑ Driver's License	❑ ID Card	
			Date Issued
❑ Oath/Affirmation	❑ Credible Witness	❑ Passport	
			Expiration Date
❑ Jurat	❑ Known Personally		
			Issuer
❑ Other_____	❑ Other: _____		

Printed Name of Witness	Signature
Address	Phone No.
	Email
Notes/Comments	Record No.

Printed Name of Signer		Signature	

Address		Phone No.	
		Email	

Date Notarized	Time	Am	Fee Charged	Travel Fee
		Pm		

Service
- ❏ Acknowledgment
- ❏ Oath/Affirmation
- ❏ Jurat
- ❏ Other_____

Satisfactory Evidence of ID
- ❏ Driver's License
- ❏ ID Card
- ❏ Credible Witness
- ❏ Passport
- ❏ Known Personally
- ❏ Other: _____

ID Number

Date Issued

Expiration Date

Issuer

Printed Name of Witness	Signature
Address	Phone No.
	Email
Notes/Comments	Record No.

Printed Name of Signer		Signature	

Address		Phone No.	
		Email	

Date Notarized	Time	Am	Fee Charged	Travel Fee
		Pm		

Service
- ❏ Acknowledgment
- ❏ Oath/Affirmation
- ❏ Jurat
- ❏ Other_____

Satisfactory Evidence of ID
- ❏ Driver's License
- ❏ ID Card
- ❏ Credible Witness
- ❏ Passport
- ❏ Known Personally
- ❏ Other: _____

ID Number

Date Issued

Expiration Date

Issuer

Printed Name of Witness	Signature
Address	Phone No.
	Email
Notes/Comments	Record No.

Printed Name of Signer		Signature	

Address	Phone No.	
	Email	

Date Notarized	Time	Am Pm	Fee Charged	Travel Fee

Service	Satisfactory Evidence of ID	ID Number
❑ Acknowledgment	❑ Driver's License ❑ ID Card	
		Date Issued
❑ Oath/Affirmation	❑ Credible Witness ❑ Passport	
		Expiration Date
❑ Jurat	❑ Known Personally	
❑ Other_____	❑ Other: _____	Issuer

Printed Name of Witness		Signature	

Address	Phone No.
	Email

Notes/Comments	Record No.

Printed Name of Signer		Signature	

Address	Phone No.	
	Email	

Date Notarized	Time	Am Pm	Fee Charged	Travel Fee

Service	Satisfactory Evidence of ID	ID Number
❑ Acknowledgment	❑ Driver's License ❑ ID Card	
		Date Issued
❑ Oath/Affirmation	❑ Credible Witness ❑ Passport	
		Expiration Date
❑ Jurat	❑ Known Personally	
❑ Other_____	❑ Other: _____	Issuer

Printed Name of Witness		Signature	

Address	Phone No.
	Email

Notes/Comments	Record No.

Printed Name of Signer		Signature	
Address		Phone No.	
		Email	

Date Notarized	Time	Am Pm	Fee Charged	Travel Fee

Service	Satisfactory Evidence of ID	ID Number
❑ Acknowledgment	❑ Driver's License ❑ ID Card	Date Issued
❑ Oath/Affirmation	❑ Credible Witness ❑ Passport	Expiration Date
❑ Jurat	❑ Known Personally	Issuer
❑ Other_____	❑ Other: _____	

Printed Name of Witness	Signature
Address	Phone No.
	Email
Notes/Comments	Record No.

Printed Name of Signer		Signature	
Address		Phone No.	
		Email	

Date Notarized	Time	Am Pm	Fee Charged	Travel Fee

Service	Satisfactory Evidence of ID	ID Number
❑ Acknowledgment	❑ Driver's License ❑ ID Card	Date Issued
❑ Oath/Affirmation	❑ Credible Witness ❑ Passport	Expiration Date
❑ Jurat	❑ Known Personally	Issuer
❑ Other_____	❑ Other: _____	

Printed Name of Witness	Signature
Address	Phone No.
	Email
Notes/Comments	Record No.

Printed Name of Signer		Signature	

Address		Phone No.	
		Email	

Date Notarized	Time	Am / Pm	Fee Charged	Travel Fee

Service	Satisfactory Evidence of ID		ID Number
❑ Acknowledgment	❑ Driver's License	❑ ID Card	
			Date Issued
❑ Oath/Affirmation	❑ Credible Witness	❑ Passport	
			Expiration Date
❑ Jurat	❑ Known Personally		
			Issuer
❑ Other_____	❑ Other: _____		

Printed Name of Witness	Signature
Address	Phone No.
	Email
Notes/Comments	Record No.

Printed Name of Signer		Signature	

Address		Phone No.	
		Email	

Date Notarized	Time	Am / Pm	Fee Charged	Travel Fee

Service	Satisfactory Evidence of ID		ID Number
❑ Acknowledgment	❑ Driver's License	❑ ID Card	
			Date Issued
❑ Oath/Affirmation	❑ Credible Witness	❑ Passport	
			Expiration Date
❑ Jurat	❑ Known Personally		
			Issuer
❑ Other_____	❑ Other: _____		

Printed Name of Witness	Signature
Address	Phone No.
	Email
Notes/Comments	Record No.

Printed Name of Signer		Signature	

Address		Phone No.	
		Email	

Date Notarized	Time	Am / Pm	Fee Charged	Travel Fee

Service	Satisfactory Evidence of ID	ID Number
❏ Acknowledgment	❏ Driver's License ❏ ID Card	
		Date Issued
❏ Oath/Affirmation	❏ Credible Witness ❏ Passport	
		Expiration Date
❏ Jurat	❏ Known Personally	
		Issuer
❏ Other_____	❏ Other: _____	

Printed Name of Witness		Signature	

Address		Phone No.	
		Email	

Notes/Comments		Record No.	

Printed Name of Signer		Signature	

Address		Phone No.	
		Email	

Date Notarized	Time	Am / Pm	Fee Charged	Travel Fee

Service	Satisfactory Evidence of ID	ID Number
❏ Acknowledgment	❏ Driver's License ❏ ID Card	
		Date Issued
❏ Oath/Affirmation	❏ Credible Witness ❏ Passport	
		Expiration Date
❏ Jurat	❏ Known Personally	
		Issuer
❏ Other_____	❏ Other: _____	

Printed Name of Witness		Signature	

Address		Phone No.	
		Email	

Notes/Comments		Record No.	

Printed Name of Signer			Signature	
Address			Phone No.	
			Email	

Date Notarized	Time	Am	Fee Charged	Travel Fee
		Pm		

Service	Satisfactory Evidence of ID		ID Number
❑ Acknowledgment	❑ Driver's License	❑ ID Card	
			Date Issued
❑ Oath/Affirmation	❑ Credible Witness	❑ Passport	
			Expiration Date
❑ Jurat	❑ Known Personally		
❑ Other_____	❑ Other: _____		Issuer

Printed Name of Witness	Signature
Address	Phone No.
	Email
Notes/Comments	Record No.

Printed Name of Signer			Signature	
Address			Phone No.	
			Email	

Date Notarized	Time	Am	Fee Charged	Travel Fee
		Pm		

Service	Satisfactory Evidence of ID		ID Number
❑ Acknowledgment	❑ Driver's License	❑ ID Card	
			Date Issued
❑ Oath/Affirmation	❑ Credible Witness	❑ Passport	
			Expiration Date
❑ Jurat	❑ Known Personally		
❑ Other_____	❑ Other: _____		Issuer

Printed Name of Witness	Signature
Address	Phone No.
	Email
Notes/Comments	Record No.

Printed Name of Signer		Signature	
Address		Phone No.	
		Email	

Date Notarized	Time	Am	Fee Charged	Travel Fee
		Pm		

Service	Satisfactory Evidence of ID		ID Number
❑ Acknowledgment	❑ Driver's License	❑ ID Card	
			Date Issued
❑ Oath/Affirmation	❑ Credible Witness	❑ Passport	
			Expiration Date
❑ Jurat	❑ Known Personally		
			Issuer
❑ Other_____	❑ Other: _____		

Printed Name of Witness	Signature
Address	Phone No.
	Email
Notes/Comments	Record No.

Printed Name of Signer		Signature	
Address		Phone No.	
		Email	

Date Notarized	Time	Am	Fee Charged	Travel Fee
		Pm		

Service	Satisfactory Evidence of ID		ID Number
❑ Acknowledgment	❑ Driver's License	❑ ID Card	
			Date Issued
❑ Oath/Affirmation	❑ Credible Witness	❑ Passport	
			Expiration Date
❑ Jurat	❑ Known Personally		
			Issuer
❑ Other_____	❑ Other: _____		

Printed Name of Witness	Signature
Address	Phone No.
	Email
Notes/Comments	Record No.

Printed Name of Signer			Signature	

Address			Phone No.	
			Email	

Date Notarized	Time	Am	Fee Charged	Travel Fee
		Pm		

Service	Satisfactory Evidence of ID		ID Number
❑ Acknowledgment	❑ Driver's License	❑ ID Card	
			Date Issued
❑ Oath/Affirmation	❑ Credible Witness	❑ Passport	
			Expiration Date
❑ Jurat	❑ Known Personally		
❑ Other_____	❑ Other: _____		Issuer

Printed Name of Witness		Signature
Address		Phone No.
		Email
Notes/Comments		Record No.

Printed Name of Signer			Signature	

Address			Phone No.	
			Email	

Date Notarized	Time	Am	Fee Charged	Travel Fee
		Pm		

Service	Satisfactory Evidence of ID		ID Number
❑ Acknowledgment	❑ Driver's License	❑ ID Card	
			Date Issued
❑ Oath/Affirmation	❑ Credible Witness	❑ Passport	
			Expiration Date
❑ Jurat	❑ Known Personally		
❑ Other_____	❑ Other: _____		Issuer

Printed Name of Witness		Signature
Address		Phone No.
		Email
Notes/Comments		Record No.

Printed Name of Signer		Signature	
Address		Phone No.	
		Email	

Date Notarized	Time	Am / Pm	Fee Charged	Travel Fee

Service	Satisfactory Evidence of ID		ID Number
❑ Acknowledgment	❑ Driver's License	❑ ID Card	
			Date Issued
❑ Oath/Affirmation	❑ Credible Witness	❑ Passport	
			Expiration Date
❑ Jurat	❑ Known Personally		
❑ Other_____	❑ Other: _____		Issuer

Printed Name of Witness		Signature
Address		Phone No.
		Email
Notes/Comments		Record No.

Printed Name of Signer		Signature	
Address		Phone No.	
		Email	

Date Notarized	Time	Am / Pm	Fee Charged	Travel Fee

Service	Satisfactory Evidence of ID		ID Number
❑ Acknowledgment	❑ Driver's License	❑ ID Card	
			Date Issued
❑ Oath/Affirmation	❑ Credible Witness	❑ Passport	
			Expiration Date
❑ Jurat	❑ Known Personally		
❑ Other_____	❑ Other: _____		Issuer

Printed Name of Witness		Signature
Address		Phone No.
		Email
Notes/Comments		Record No.

Printed Name of Signer		Signature	
Address		Phone No.	
		Email	

Date Notarized	Time	Am	Fee Charged	Travel Fee
		Pm		

Service	Satisfactory Evidence of ID		ID Number
❏ Acknowledgment	❏ Driver's License	❏ ID Card	
			Date Issued
❏ Oath/Affirmation	❏ Credible Witness	❏ Passport	
			Expiration Date
❏ Jurat	❏ Known Personally		
❏ Other_____	❏ Other: _____		Issuer

Printed Name of Witness		Signature	
Address		Phone No.	
		Email	
Notes/Comments		Record No.	

Printed Name of Signer		Signature	
Address		Phone No.	
		Email	

Date Notarized	Time	Am	Fee Charged	Travel Fee
		Pm		

Service	Satisfactory Evidence of ID		ID Number
❏ Acknowledgment	❏ Driver's License	❏ ID Card	
			Date Issued
❏ Oath/Affirmation	❏ Credible Witness	❏ Passport	
			Expiration Date
❏ Jurat	❏ Known Personally		
❏ Other_____	❏ Other: _____		Issuer

Printed Name of Witness		Signature	
Address		Phone No.	
		Email	
Notes/Comments		Record No.	

Printed Name of Signer		Signature	
Address		Phone No.	
		Email	

Date Notarized	Time	Am / Pm	Fee Charged	Travel Fee

Service	Satisfactory Evidence of ID		ID Number
❏ Acknowledgment	❏ Driver's License	❏ ID Card	
❏ Oath/Affirmation	❏ Credible Witness	❏ Passport	Date Issued
❏ Jurat	❏ Known Personally		Expiration Date
❏ Other_____	❏ Other: _____		Issuer

Printed Name of Witness	Signature
Address	Phone No.
	Email
Notes/Comments	Record No.

Printed Name of Signer		Signature	
Address		Phone No.	
		Email	

Date Notarized	Time	Am / Pm	Fee Charged	Travel Fee

Service	Satisfactory Evidence of ID		ID Number
❏ Acknowledgment	❏ Driver's License	❏ ID Card	
❏ Oath/Affirmation	❏ Credible Witness	❏ Passport	Date Issued
❏ Jurat	❏ Known Personally		Expiration Date
❏ Other_____	❏ Other: _____		Issuer

Printed Name of Witness	Signature
Address	Phone No.
	Email
Notes/Comments	Record No.

Printed Name of Signer		Signature	
Address		Phone No.	
		Email	

Date Notarized	Time	Am Pm	Fee Charged	Travel Fee

Service	Satisfactory Evidence of ID		ID Number
❏ Acknowledgment	❏ Driver's License	❏ ID Card	
			Date Issued
❏ Oath/Affirmation	❏ Credible Witness	❏ Passport	
			Expiration Date
❏ Jurat	❏ Known Personally		
			Issuer
❏ Other_____	❏ Other: _____		

Printed Name of Witness	Signature
Address	Phone No.
	Email
Notes/Comments	Record No.

Printed Name of Signer		Signature	
Address		Phone No.	
		Email	

Date Notarized	Time	Am Pm	Fee Charged	Travel Fee

Service	Satisfactory Evidence of ID		ID Number
❏ Acknowledgment	❏ Driver's License	❏ ID Card	
			Date Issued
❏ Oath/Affirmation	❏ Credible Witness	❏ Passport	
			Expiration Date
❏ Jurat	❏ Known Personally		
			Issuer
❏ Other_____	❏ Other: _____		

Printed Name of Witness	Signature
Address	Phone No.
	Email
Notes/Comments	Record No.

Printed Name of Signer		Signature	

Address		Phone No.	
		Email	

Date Notarized	Time	Am / Pm	Fee Charged	Travel Fee

Service	Satisfactory Evidence of ID	ID Number
❑ Acknowledgment	❑ Driver's License ❑ ID Card	Date Issued
❑ Oath/Affirmation	❑ Credible Witness ❑ Passport	Expiration Date
❑ Jurat	❑ Known Personally	Issuer
❑ Other_____	❑ Other: _____	

Printed Name of Witness		Signature
Address		Phone No.
		Email
Notes/Comments		Record No.

Printed Name of Signer		Signature	

Address		Phone No.	
		Email	

Date Notarized	Time	Am / Pm	Fee Charged	Travel Fee

Service	Satisfactory Evidence of ID	ID Number
❑ Acknowledgment	❑ Driver's License ❑ ID Card	Date Issued
❑ Oath/Affirmation	❑ Credible Witness ❑ Passport	Expiration Date
❑ Jurat	❑ Known Personally	Issuer
❑ Other_____	❑ Other: _____	

Printed Name of Witness		Signature
Address		Phone No.
		Email
Notes/Comments		Record No.

Printed Name of Signer		Signature	

Address		Phone No.	
		Email	

Date Notarized	Time	Am	Fee Charged	Travel Fee
		Pm		

Service	Satisfactory Evidence of ID		ID Number
❑ Acknowledgment	❑ Driver's License	❑ ID Card	
			Date Issued
❑ Oath/Affirmation	❑ Credible Witness	❑ Passport	
			Expiration Date
❑ Jurat	❑ Known Personally		
❑ Other_____	❑ Other: _____		Issuer

Printed Name of Witness	Signature
Address	Phone No.
	Email
Notes/Comments	Record No.

Printed Name of Signer		Signature	

Address		Phone No.	
		Email	

Date Notarized	Time	Am	Fee Charged	Travel Fee
		Pm		

Service	Satisfactory Evidence of ID		ID Number
❑ Acknowledgment	❑ Driver's License	❑ ID Card	
			Date Issued
❑ Oath/Affirmation	❑ Credible Witness	❑ Passport	
			Expiration Date
❑ Jurat	❑ Known Personally		
❑ Other_____	❑ Other: _____		Issuer

Printed Name of Witness	Signature
Address	Phone No.
	Email
Notes/Comments	Record No.

Printed Name of Signer		Signature	
Address		**Phone No.**	
		Email	

Date Notarized	Time	Am	Fee Charged	Travel Fee
		Pm		

Service	Satisfactory Evidence of ID		ID Number
❑ Acknowledgment	❑ Driver's License	❑ ID Card	Date Issued
❑ Oath/Affirmation	❑ Credible Witness	❑ Passport	Expiration Date
❑ Jurat	❑ Known Personally		Issuer
❑ Other_____	❑ Other: _____		

Printed Name of Witness	Signature
Address	**Phone No.**
	Email
Notes/Comments	**Record No.**

Printed Name of Signer		Signature	
Address		**Phone No.**	
		Email	

Date Notarized	Time	Am	Fee Charged	Travel Fee
		Pm		

Service	Satisfactory Evidence of ID		ID Number
❑ Acknowledgment	❑ Driver's License	❑ ID Card	Date Issued
❑ Oath/Affirmation	❑ Credible Witness	❑ Passport	Expiration Date
❑ Jurat	❑ Known Personally		Issuer
❑ Other_____	❑ Other: _____		

Printed Name of Witness	Signature
Address	**Phone No.**
	Email
Notes/Comments	**Record No.**

Printed Name of Signer		Signature	
Address		Phone No.	
		Email	

Date Notarized	Time	Am	Fee Charged	Travel Fee
		Pm		

Service	Satisfactory Evidence of ID		ID Number
❑ Acknowledgment	❑ Driver's License	❑ ID Card	
			Date Issued
❑ Oath/Affirmation	❑ Credible Witness	❑ Passport	Expiration Date
❑ Jurat	❑ Known Personally		Issuer
❑ Other_____	❑ Other: _____		

Printed Name of Witness	Signature
Address	Phone No.
	Email
Notes/Comments	Record No.

Printed Name of Signer		Signature	
Address		Phone No.	
		Email	

Date Notarized	Time	Am	Fee Charged	Travel Fee
		Pm		

Service	Satisfactory Evidence of ID		ID Number
❑ Acknowledgment	❑ Driver's License	❑ ID Card	
			Date Issued
❑ Oath/Affirmation	❑ Credible Witness	❑ Passport	Expiration Date
❑ Jurat	❑ Known Personally		Issuer
❑ Other_____	❑ Other: _____		

Printed Name of Witness	Signature
Address	Phone No.
	Email
Notes/Comments	Record No.

Printed Name of Signer		Signature	
Address		Phone No.	
		Email	

Date Notarized	Time	Am / Pm	Fee Charged	Travel Fee

Service	Satisfactory Evidence of ID		ID Number
❏ Acknowledgment	❏ Driver's License	❏ ID Card	
			Date Issued
❏ Oath/Affirmation	❏ Credible Witness	❏ Passport	
			Expiration Date
❏ Jurat	❏ Known Personally		
❏ Other_____	❏ Other: _____		Issuer

Printed Name of Witness		Signature
Address		Phone No.
		Email
Notes/Comments		Record No.

Printed Name of Signer		Signature	
Address		Phone No.	
		Email	

Date Notarized	Time	Am / Pm	Fee Charged	Travel Fee

Service	Satisfactory Evidence of ID		ID Number
❏ Acknowledgment	❏ Driver's License	❏ ID Card	
			Date Issued
❏ Oath/Affirmation	❏ Credible Witness	❏ Passport	
			Expiration Date
❏ Jurat	❏ Known Personally		
❏ Other_____	❏ Other: _____		Issuer

Printed Name of Witness		Signature
Address		Phone No.
		Email
Notes/Comments		Record No.

Printed Name of Signer		Signature	
Address		Phone No.	
		Email	

Date Notarized	Time	Am	Fee Charged	Travel Fee
		Pm		

Service	Satisfactory Evidence of ID		ID Number
❑ Acknowledgment	❑ Driver's License	❑ ID Card	
			Date Issued
❑ Oath/Affirmation	❑ Credible Witness	❑ Passport	
			Expiration Date
❑ Jurat	❑ Known Personally		
			Issuer
❑ Other_____	❑ Other: _____		

Printed Name of Witness	Signature
Address	Phone No.
	Email
Notes/Comments	Record No.

Printed Name of Signer		Signature	
Address		Phone No.	
		Email	

Date Notarized	Time	Am	Fee Charged	Travel Fee
		Pm		

Service	Satisfactory Evidence of ID		ID Number
❑ Acknowledgment	❑ Driver's License	❑ ID Card	
			Date Issued
❑ Oath/Affirmation	❑ Credible Witness	❑ Passport	
			Expiration Date
❑ Jurat	❑ Known Personally		
			Issuer
❑ Other_____	❑ Other: _____		

Printed Name of Witness	Signature
Address	Phone No.
	Email
Notes/Comments	Record No.

Printed Name of Signer		Signature	
Address		Phone No.	
		Email	

Date Notarized	Time	Am Pm	Fee Charged	Travel Fee

Service	Satisfactory Evidence of ID		ID Number
❑ Acknowledgment	❑ Driver's License	❑ ID Card	Date Issued
❑ Oath/Affirmation	❑ Credible Witness	❑ Passport	Expiration Date
❑ Jurat	❑ Known Personally		Issuer
❑ Other_____	❑ Other: _____		

Printed Name of Witness	Signature
Address	Phone No.
	Email
Notes/Comments	Record No.

Printed Name of Signer		Signature	
Address		Phone No.	
		Email	

Date Notarized	Time	Am Pm	Fee Charged	Travel Fee

Service	Satisfactory Evidence of ID		ID Number
❑ Acknowledgment	❑ Driver's License	❑ ID Card	Date Issued
❑ Oath/Affirmation	❑ Credible Witness	❑ Passport	Expiration Date
❑ Jurat	❑ Known Personally		Issuer
❑ Other_____	❑ Other: _____		

Printed Name of Witness	Signature
Address	Phone No.
	Email
Notes/Comments	Record No.

Printed Name of Signer		Signature	
Address		Phone No.	
		Email	

Date Notarized	Time	Am	Fee Charged	Travel Fee
		Pm		

Service	Satisfactory Evidence of ID		ID Number
❑ Acknowledgment	❑ Driver's License	❑ ID Card	
			Date Issued
❑ Oath/Affirmation	❑ Credible Witness	❑ Passport	
			Expiration Date
❑ Jurat	❑ Known Personally		
			Issuer
❑ Other_____	❑ Other: _____		

Printed Name of Witness	Signature
Address	Phone No.
	Email
Notes/Comments	Record No.

Printed Name of Signer		Signature	
Address		Phone No.	
		Email	

Date Notarized	Time	Am	Fee Charged	Travel Fee
		Pm		

Service	Satisfactory Evidence of ID		ID Number
❑ Acknowledgment	❑ Driver's License	❑ ID Card	
			Date Issued
❑ Oath/Affirmation	❑ Credible Witness	❑ Passport	
			Expiration Date
❑ Jurat	❑ Known Personally		
			Issuer
❑ Other_____	❑ Other: _____		

Printed Name of Witness	Signature
Address	Phone No.
	Email
Notes/Comments	Record No.

Printed Name of Signer		Signature	
Address		Phone No.	
		Email	

Date Notarized	Time	Am Pm	Fee Charged	Travel Fee

Service	Satisfactory Evidence of ID	ID Number
❑ Acknowledgment	❑ Driver's License ❑ ID Card	Date Issued
❑ Oath/Affirmation	❑ Credible Witness ❑ Passport	Expiration Date
❑ Jurat	❑ Known Personally	Issuer
❑ Other_____	❑ Other: _____	

Printed Name of Witness		Signature
Address		Phone No.
		Email
Notes/Comments		Record No.

Printed Name of Signer		Signature	
Address		Phone No.	
		Email	

Date Notarized	Time	Am Pm	Fee Charged	Travel Fee

Service	Satisfactory Evidence of ID	ID Number
❑ Acknowledgment	❑ Driver's License ❑ ID Card	Date Issued
❑ Oath/Affirmation	❑ Credible Witness ❑ Passport	Expiration Date
❑ Jurat	❑ Known Personally	Issuer
❑ Other_____	❑ Other: _____	

Printed Name of Witness		Signature
Address		Phone No.
		Email
Notes/Comments		Record No.

Printed Name of Signer		Signature	
Address		Phone No.	
		Email	

Date Notarized	Time	Am	Fee Charged	Travel Fee
		Pm		

Service	Satisfactory Evidence of ID		ID Number
❏ Acknowledgment	❏ Driver's License	❏ ID Card	Date Issued
❏ Oath/Affirmation	❏ Credible Witness	❏ Passport	Expiration Date
❏ Jurat	❏ Known Personally		Issuer
❏ Other_____	❏ Other: _____		

Printed Name of Witness	Signature
Address	Phone No.
	Email
Notes/Comments	Record No.

Printed Name of Signer		Signature	
Address		Phone No.	
		Email	

Date Notarized	Time	Am	Fee Charged	Travel Fee
		Pm		

Service	Satisfactory Evidence of ID		ID Number
❏ Acknowledgment	❏ Driver's License	❏ ID Card	Date Issued
❏ Oath/Affirmation	❏ Credible Witness	❏ Passport	Expiration Date
❏ Jurat	❏ Known Personally		Issuer
❏ Other_____	❏ Other: _____		

Printed Name of Witness	Signature
Address	Phone No.
	Email
Notes/Comments	Record No.

Printed Name of Signer		Signature	

Address		Phone No.	
		Email	

Date Notarized	Time	Am Pm	Fee Charged	Travel Fee

Service	Satisfactory Evidence of ID	ID Number
❑ Acknowledgment	❑ Driver's License ❑ ID Card	
		Date Issued
❑ Oath/Affirmation	❑ Credible Witness ❑ Passport	
		Expiration Date
❑ Jurat	❑ Known Personally	
		Issuer
❑ Other_____	❑ Other: _____	

Printed Name of Witness		Signature

Address		Phone No.
		Email

Notes/Comments		Record No.

Printed Name of Signer		Signature	

Address		Phone No.	
		Email	

Date Notarized	Time	Am Pm	Fee Charged	Travel Fee

Service	Satisfactory Evidence of ID	ID Number
❑ Acknowledgment	❑ Driver's License ❑ ID Card	
		Date Issued
❑ Oath/Affirmation	❑ Credible Witness ❑ Passport	
		Expiration Date
❑ Jurat	❑ Known Personally	
		Issuer
❑ Other_____	❑ Other: _____	

Printed Name of Witness		Signature

Address		Phone No.
		Email

Notes/Comments		Record No.

Printed Name of Signer		Signature	

Address	Phone No.
	Email

Date Notarized	Time	Am	Fee Charged	Travel Fee
		Pm		

Service	Satisfactory Evidence of ID		ID Number
❑ Acknowledgment	❑ Driver's License	❑ ID Card	
			Date Issued
❑ Oath/Affirmation	❑ Credible Witness	❑ Passport	
			Expiration Date
❑ Jurat	❑ Known Personally		
❑ Other_____	❑ Other: _____		Issuer

Printed Name of Witness	Signature

Address	Phone No.
	Email

Notes/Comments	Record No.

Printed Name of Signer		Signature	

Address	Phone No.
	Email

Date Notarized	Time	Am	Fee Charged	Travel Fee
		Pm		

Service	Satisfactory Evidence of ID		ID Number
❑ Acknowledgment	❑ Driver's License	❑ ID Card	
			Date Issued
❑ Oath/Affirmation	❑ Credible Witness	❑ Passport	
			Expiration Date
❑ Jurat	❑ Known Personally		
❑ Other_____	❑ Other: _____		Issuer

Printed Name of Witness	Signature

Address	Phone No.
	Email

Notes/Comments	Record No.

Printed Name of Signer		Signature	

Address	Phone No.	
	Email	

Date Notarized	Time	Am / Pm	Fee Charged	Travel Fee

Service	Satisfactory Evidence of ID		ID Number
❏ Acknowledgment	❏ Driver's License	❏ ID Card	
			Date Issued
❏ Oath/Affirmation	❏ Credible Witness	❏ Passport	
			Expiration Date
❏ Jurat	❏ Known Personally		
❏ Other_____	❏ Other: _____		Issuer

Printed Name of Witness	Signature

Address	Phone No.
	Email

Notes/Comments	Record No.

Printed Name of Signer		Signature	

Address	Phone No.	
	Email	

Date Notarized	Time	Am / Pm	Fee Charged	Travel Fee

Service	Satisfactory Evidence of ID		ID Number
❏ Acknowledgment	❏ Driver's License	❏ ID Card	
			Date Issued
❏ Oath/Affirmation	❏ Credible Witness	❏ Passport	
			Expiration Date
❏ Jurat	❏ Known Personally		
❏ Other_____	❏ Other: _____		Issuer

Printed Name of Witness	Signature

Address	Phone No.
	Email

Notes/Comments	Record No.

Printed Name of Signer		Signature	
Address		Phone No.	
		Email	

Date Notarized	Time	Am	Fee Charged	Travel Fee
		Pm		

Service	Satisfactory Evidence of ID		ID Number
❑ Acknowledgment	❑ Driver's License	❑ ID Card	
			Date Issued
❑ Oath/Affirmation	❑ Credible Witness	❑ Passport	
			Expiration Date
❑ Jurat	❑ Known Personally		
			Issuer
❑ Other_____	❑ Other: _____		

Printed Name of Witness	Signature
Address	Phone No.
	Email
Notes/Comments	Record No.

Printed Name of Signer		Signature	
Address		Phone No.	
		Email	

Date Notarized	Time	Am	Fee Charged	Travel Fee
		Pm		

Service	Satisfactory Evidence of ID		ID Number
❑ Acknowledgment	❑ Driver's License	❑ ID Card	
			Date Issued
❑ Oath/Affirmation	❑ Credible Witness	❑ Passport	
			Expiration Date
❑ Jurat	❑ Known Personally		
			Issuer
❑ Other_____	❑ Other: _____		

Printed Name of Witness	Signature
Address	Phone No.
	Email
Notes/Comments	Record No.

Printed Name of Signer		Signature	
Address		**Phone No.**	
		Email	
Date Notarized	**Time** **Am** **Pm**	**Fee Charged**	**Travel Fee**

Service	Satisfactory Evidence of ID		ID Number
❑ Acknowledgment	❑ Driver's License	❑ ID Card	Date Issued
❑ Oath/Affirmation	❑ Credible Witness	❑ Passport	Expiration Date
❑ Jurat	❑ Known Personally		Issuer
❑ Other_____	❑ Other: _____		

Printed Name of Witness	Signature
Address	**Phone No.**
	Email
Notes/Comments	**Record No.**

Printed Name of Signer		Signature	
Address		**Phone No.**	
		Email	
Date Notarized	**Time** **Am** **Pm**	**Fee Charged**	**Travel Fee**

Service	Satisfactory Evidence of ID		ID Number
❑ Acknowledgment	❑ Driver's License	❑ ID Card	Date Issued
❑ Oath/Affirmation	❑ Credible Witness	❑ Passport	Expiration Date
❑ Jurat	❑ Known Personally		Issuer
❑ Other_____	❑ Other: _____		

Printed Name of Witness	Signature
Address	**Phone No.**
	Email
Notes/Comments	**Record No.**

Printed Name of Signer			Signature	
Address			Phone No.	
			Email	
Date Notarized	Time	Am Pm	Fee Charged	Travel Fee

Service	Satisfactory Evidence of ID		ID Number
❑ Acknowledgment	❑ Driver's License	❑ ID Card	
			Date Issued
❑ Oath/Affirmation	❑ Credible Witness	❑ Passport	
			Expiration Date
❑ Jurat	❑ Known Personally		
❑ Other_____	❑ Other: _____		Issuer

Printed Name of Witness	Signature
Address	Phone No.
	Email
Notes/Comments	Record No.

Printed Name of Signer			Signature	
Address			Phone No.	
			Email	
Date Notarized	Time	Am Pm	Fee Charged	Travel Fee

Service	Satisfactory Evidence of ID		ID Number
❑ Acknowledgment	❑ Driver's License	❑ ID Card	
			Date Issued
❑ Oath/Affirmation	❑ Credible Witness	❑ Passport	
			Expiration Date
❑ Jurat	❑ Known Personally		
❑ Other_____	❑ Other: _____		Issuer

Printed Name of Witness	Signature
Address	Phone No.
	Email
Notes/Comments	Record No.

Printed Name of Signer		Signature	
Address		Phone No.	
		Email	

Date Notarized	Time	Am	Fee Charged	Travel Fee
		Pm		

Service	Satisfactory Evidence of ID		ID Number
❑ Acknowledgment	❑ Driver's License	❑ ID Card	
			Date Issued
❑ Oath/Affirmation	❑ Credible Witness	❑ Passport	Expiration Date
❑ Jurat	❑ Known Personally		Issuer
❑ Other_____	❑ Other: _____		

Printed Name of Witness	Signature
Address	Phone No.
	Email
Notes/Comments	Record No.

Printed Name of Signer		Signature	
Address		Phone No.	
		Email	

Date Notarized	Time	Am	Fee Charged	Travel Fee
		Pm		

Service	Satisfactory Evidence of ID		ID Number
❑ Acknowledgment	❑ Driver's License	❑ ID Card	
			Date Issued
❑ Oath/Affirmation	❑ Credible Witness	❑ Passport	Expiration Date
❑ Jurat	❑ Known Personally		Issuer
❑ Other_____	❑ Other: _____		

Printed Name of Witness	Signature
Address	Phone No.
	Email
Notes/Comments	Record No.

Printed Name of Signer		Signature	

Address		Phone No.	
		Email	

Date Notarized	Time	Am	Fee Charged	Travel Fee
		Pm		

Service	Satisfactory Evidence of ID		ID Number
❏ Acknowledgment	❏ Driver's License	❏ ID Card	
			Date Issued
❏ Oath/Affirmation	❏ Credible Witness	❏ Passport	
			Expiration Date
❏ Jurat	❏ Known Personally		
			Issuer
❏ Other_____	❏ Other: _____		

Printed Name of Witness	Signature
Address	Phone No.
	Email
Notes/Comments	Record No.

Printed Name of Signer		Signature	

Address		Phone No.	
		Email	

Date Notarized	Time	Am	Fee Charged	Travel Fee
		Pm		

Service	Satisfactory Evidence of ID		ID Number
❏ Acknowledgment	❏ Driver's License	❏ ID Card	
			Date Issued
❏ Oath/Affirmation	❏ Credible Witness	❏ Passport	
			Expiration Date
❏ Jurat	❏ Known Personally		
			Issuer
❏ Other_____	❏ Other: _____		

Printed Name of Witness	Signature
Address	Phone No.
	Email
Notes/Comments	Record No.

Printed Name of Signer			Signature	
Address		Phone No.		
		Email		
Date Notarized	Time	Am Pm	Fee Charged	Travel Fee

Service	Satisfactory Evidence of ID		ID Number
❑ Acknowledgment	❑ Driver's License	❑ ID Card	Date Issued
❑ Oath/Affirmation	❑ Credible Witness	❑ Passport	Expiration Date
❑ Jurat	❑ Known Personally		Issuer
❑ Other_____	❑ Other: _____		

Printed Name of Witness	Signature
Address	Phone No.
	Email
Notes/Comments	Record No.

Printed Name of Signer			Signature	
Address		Phone No.		
		Email		
Date Notarized	Time	Am Pm	Fee Charged	Travel Fee

Service	Satisfactory Evidence of ID		ID Number
❑ Acknowledgment	❑ Driver's License	❑ ID Card	Date Issued
❑ Oath/Affirmation	❑ Credible Witness	❑ Passport	Expiration Date
❑ Jurat	❑ Known Personally		Issuer
❑ Other_____	❑ Other: _____		

Printed Name of Witness	Signature
Address	Phone No.
	Email
Notes/Comments	Record No.

Printed Name of Signer			Signature	
Address			Phone No.	
			Email	
Date Notarized	Time	Am Pm	Fee Charged	Travel Fee

Service	Satisfactory Evidence of ID		ID Number
❑ Acknowledgment	❑ Driver's License	❑ ID Card	Date Issued
❑ Oath/Affirmation	❑ Credible Witness	❑ Passport	Expiration Date
❑ Jurat	❑ Known Personally		Issuer
❑ Other_____	❑ Other: _____		

Printed Name of Witness	Signature
Address	Phone No.
	Email
Notes/Comments	Record No.

Printed Name of Signer			Signature	
Address			Phone No.	
			Email	
Date Notarized	Time	Am Pm	Fee Charged	Travel Fee

Service	Satisfactory Evidence of ID		ID Number
❑ Acknowledgment	❑ Driver's License	❑ ID Card	Date Issued
❑ Oath/Affirmation	❑ Credible Witness	❑ Passport	Expiration Date
❑ Jurat	❑ Known Personally		Issuer
❑ Other_____	❑ Other: _____		

Printed Name of Witness	Signature
Address	Phone No.
	Email
Notes/Comments	Record No.

Printed Name of Signer		Signature	
Address		**Phone No.**	
		Email	

Date Notarized	Time	Am Pm	Fee Charged	Travel Fee

Service	Satisfactory Evidence of ID	ID Number
❑ Acknowledgment	❑ Driver's License ❑ ID Card	
		Date Issued
❑ Oath/Affirmation	❑ Credible Witness ❑ Passport	
		Expiration Date
❑ Jurat	❑ Known Personally	
❑ Other_____	❑ Other: _____	Issuer

Printed Name of Witness	Signature
Address	**Phone No.**
	Email
Notes/Comments	**Record No.**

Printed Name of Signer		Signature	
Address		**Phone No.**	
		Email	

Date Notarized	Time	Am Pm	Fee Charged	Travel Fee

Service	Satisfactory Evidence of ID	ID Number
❑ Acknowledgment	❑ Driver's License ❑ ID Card	
		Date Issued
❑ Oath/Affirmation	❑ Credible Witness ❑ Passport	
		Expiration Date
❑ Jurat	❑ Known Personally	
❑ Other_____	❑ Other: _____	Issuer

Printed Name of Witness	Signature
Address	**Phone No.**
	Email
Notes/Comments	**Record No.**

Printed Name of Signer		Signature	
Address		Phone No.	
		Email	

Date Notarized	Time	Am	Fee Charged	Travel Fee
		Pm		

Service	Satisfactory Evidence of ID		ID Number
❑ Acknowledgment	❑ Driver's License	❑ ID Card	
			Date Issued
❑ Oath/Affirmation	❑ Credible Witness	❑ Passport	
			Expiration Date
❑ Jurat	❑ Known Personally		
❑ Other_____	❑ Other: _____		Issuer

Printed Name of Witness		Signature
Address		Phone No.
		Email
Notes/Comments		Record No.

Printed Name of Signer		Signature	
Address		Phone No.	
		Email	

Date Notarized	Time	Am	Fee Charged	Travel Fee
		Pm		

Service	Satisfactory Evidence of ID		ID Number
❑ Acknowledgment	❑ Driver's License	❑ ID Card	
			Date Issued
❑ Oath/Affirmation	❑ Credible Witness	❑ Passport	
			Expiration Date
❑ Jurat	❑ Known Personally		
❑ Other_____	❑ Other: _____		Issuer

Printed Name of Witness		Signature
Address		Phone No.
		Email
Notes/Comments		Record No.

Printed Name of Signer			Signature	
Address			Phone No.	
			Email	

Date Notarized	Time	Am	Fee Charged	Travel Fee
		Pm		

Service	Satisfactory Evidence of ID		ID Number
❑ Acknowledgment	❑ Driver's License	❑ ID Card	Date Issued
❑ Oath/Affirmation	❑ Credible Witness	❑ Passport	Expiration Date
❑ Jurat	❑ Known Personally		Issuer
❑ Other_____	❑ Other: _____		

Printed Name of Witness	Signature
Address	Phone No.
	Email
Notes/Comments	Record No.

Printed Name of Signer			Signature	
Address			Phone No.	
			Email	

Date Notarized	Time	Am	Fee Charged	Travel Fee
		Pm		

Service	Satisfactory Evidence of ID		ID Number
❑ Acknowledgment	❑ Driver's License	❑ ID Card	Date Issued
❑ Oath/Affirmation	❑ Credible Witness	❑ Passport	Expiration Date
❑ Jurat	❑ Known Personally		Issuer
❑ Other_____	❑ Other: _____		

Printed Name of Witness	Signature
Address	Phone No.
	Email
Notes/Comments	Record No.

Printed Name of Signer		Signature	
Address		Phone No.	
		Email	
Date Notarized	Time Am Pm	Fee Charged	Travel Fee

Service	Satisfactory Evidence of ID		ID Number
❑ Acknowledgment	❑ Driver's License	❑ ID Card	Date Issued
❑ Oath/Affirmation	❑ Credible Witness	❑ Passport	Expiration Date
❑ Jurat	❑ Known Personally		Issuer
❑ Other_____	❑ Other: _____		

Printed Name of Witness	Signature
Address	Phone No.
	Email
Notes/Comments	Record No.

Printed Name of Signer		Signature	
Address		Phone No.	
		Email	
Date Notarized	Time Am Pm	Fee Charged	Travel Fee

Service	Satisfactory Evidence of ID		ID Number
❑ Acknowledgment	❑ Driver's License	❑ ID Card	Date Issued
❑ Oath/Affirmation	❑ Credible Witness	❑ Passport	Expiration Date
❑ Jurat	❑ Known Personally		Issuer
❑ Other_____	❑ Other: _____		

Printed Name of Witness	Signature
Address	Phone No.
	Email
Notes/Comments	Record No.

Printed Name of Signer				Signature	

Address			Phone No.	
			Email	

Date Notarized	Time	Am	Fee Charged	Travel Fee
		Pm		

Service

❑ Acknowledgment

❑ Oath/Affirmation

❑ Jurat

❑ Other_____

Satisfactory Evidence of ID

❑ Driver's License ❑ ID Card

❑ Credible Witness ❑ Passport

❑ Known Personally

❑ Other: _____

ID Number

Date Issued

Expiration Date

Issuer

Printed Name of Witness	Signature
Address	Phone No.
	Email
Notes/Comments	Record No.

Printed Name of Signer				Signature	

Address			Phone No.	
			Email	

Date Notarized	Time	Am	Fee Charged	Travel Fee
		Pm		

Service

❑ Acknowledgment

❑ Oath/Affirmation

❑ Jurat

❑ Other_____

Satisfactory Evidence of ID

❑ Driver's License ❑ ID Card

❑ Credible Witness ❑ Passport

❑ Known Personally

❑ Other: _____

ID Number

Date Issued

Expiration Date

Issuer

Printed Name of Witness	Signature
Address	Phone No.
	Email
Notes/Comments	Record No.

Printed Name of Signer		Signature	
Address		Phone No.	
		Email	

Date Notarized	Time	Am	Fee Charged	Travel Fee
		Pm		

Service	Satisfactory Evidence of ID		ID Number
❑ Acknowledgment	❑ Driver's License	❑ ID Card	Date Issued
❑ Oath/Affirmation	❑ Credible Witness	❑ Passport	Expiration Date
❑ Jurat	❑ Known Personally		Issuer
❑ Other_____	❑ Other: _____		

Printed Name of Witness		Signature	
Address		Phone No.	
		Email	
Notes/Comments		Record No.	

Printed Name of Signer		Signature	
Address		Phone No.	
		Email	

Date Notarized	Time	Am	Fee Charged	Travel Fee
		Pm		

Service	Satisfactory Evidence of ID		ID Number
❑ Acknowledgment	❑ Driver's License	❑ ID Card	Date Issued
❑ Oath/Affirmation	❑ Credible Witness	❑ Passport	Expiration Date
❑ Jurat	❑ Known Personally		Issuer
❑ Other_____	❑ Other: _____		

Printed Name of Witness		Signature	
Address		Phone No.	
		Email	
Notes/Comments		Record No.	

Printed Name of Signer		Signature	
Address		Phone No.	
		Email	

Date Notarized	Time	Am / Pm	Fee Charged	Travel Fee

Service	Satisfactory Evidence of ID		ID Number
❑ Acknowledgment	❑ Driver's License	❑ ID Card	Date Issued
❑ Oath/Affirmation	❑ Credible Witness	❑ Passport	Expiration Date
❑ Jurat	❑ Known Personally		Issuer
❑ Other_____	❑ Other: _____		

Printed Name of Witness		Signature	
Address		Phone No.	
		Email	
Notes/Comments		Record No.	

Printed Name of Signer		Signature	
Address		Phone No.	
		Email	

Date Notarized	Time	Am / Pm	Fee Charged	Travel Fee

Service	Satisfactory Evidence of ID		ID Number
❑ Acknowledgment	❑ Driver's License	❑ ID Card	Date Issued
❑ Oath/Affirmation	❑ Credible Witness	❑ Passport	Expiration Date
❑ Jurat	❑ Known Personally		Issuer
❑ Other_____	❑ Other: _____		

Printed Name of Witness		Signature	
Address		Phone No.	
		Email	
Notes/Comments		Record No.	

Printed Name of Signer		Signature	
Address		Phone No.	
		Email	

Date Notarized	Time	Am Pm	Fee Charged	Travel Fee

Service

- ❑ Acknowledgment
- ❑ Oath/Affirmation
- ❑ Jurat
- ❑ Other_____

Satisfactory Evidence of ID

- ❑ Driver's License
- ❑ ID Card
- ❑ Credible Witness
- ❑ Passport
- ❑ Known Personally
- ❑ Other: _____

ID Number

Date Issued

Expiration Date

Issuer

Printed Name of Witness	Signature
Address	Phone No.
	Email
Notes/Comments	**Record No.**

Printed Name of Signer		Signature	
Address		Phone No.	
		Email	

Date Notarized	Time	Am Pm	Fee Charged	Travel Fee

Service

- ❑ Acknowledgment
- ❑ Oath/Affirmation
- ❑ Jurat
- ❑ Other_____

Satisfactory Evidence of ID

- ❑ Driver's License
- ❑ ID Card
- ❑ Credible Witness
- ❑ Passport
- ❑ Known Personally
- ❑ Other: _____

ID Number

Date Issued

Expiration Date

Issuer

Printed Name of Witness	Signature
Address	Phone No.
	Email
Notes/Comments	**Record No.**

Printed Name of Signer		Signature		
Address		Phone No.		
		Email		

Date Notarized	Time	Am	Fee Charged	Travel Fee
		Pm		

Service	Satisfactory Evidence of ID		ID Number
❑ Acknowledgment	❑ Driver's License	❑ ID Card	
			Date Issued
❑ Oath/Affirmation	❑ Credible Witness	❑ Passport	Expiration Date
❑ Jurat	❑ Known Personally		Issuer
❑ Other_____	❑ Other: _____		

Printed Name of Witness		Signature
Address		Phone No.
		Email
Notes/Comments		Record No.

Printed Name of Signer		Signature		
Address		Phone No.		
		Email		

Date Notarized	Time	Am	Fee Charged	Travel Fee
		Pm		

Service	Satisfactory Evidence of ID		ID Number
❑ Acknowledgment	❑ Driver's License	❑ ID Card	
			Date Issued
❑ Oath/Affirmation	❑ Credible Witness	❑ Passport	Expiration Date
❑ Jurat	❑ Known Personally		Issuer
❑ Other_____	❑ Other: _____		

Printed Name of Witness		Signature
Address		Phone No.
		Email
Notes/Comments		Record No.

Printed Name of Signer		Signature	
Address		Phone No.	
		Email	

Date Notarized	Time	Am	Fee Charged	Travel Fee
		Pm		

Service	Satisfactory Evidence of ID		ID Number
☐ Acknowledgment	☐ Driver's License	☐ ID Card	Date Issued
☐ Oath/Affirmation	☐ Credible Witness	☐ Passport	Expiration Date
☐ Jurat	☐ Known Personally		Issuer
☐ Other_____	☐ Other: _____		

Printed Name of Witness		Signature
Address		Phone No.
		Email
Notes/Comments		Record No.

Printed Name of Signer		Signature	
Address		Phone No.	
		Email	

Date Notarized	Time	Am	Fee Charged	Travel Fee
		Pm		

Service	Satisfactory Evidence of ID		ID Number
☐ Acknowledgment	☐ Driver's License	☐ ID Card	Date Issued
☐ Oath/Affirmation	☐ Credible Witness	☐ Passport	Expiration Date
☐ Jurat	☐ Known Personally		Issuer
☐ Other_____	☐ Other: _____		

Printed Name of Witness		Signature
Address		Phone No.
		Email
Notes/Comments		Record No.

Printed Name of Signer		Signature	
Address		Phone No.	
		Email	

Date Notarized	Time	Am	Fee Charged	Travel Fee
		Pm		

Service	Satisfactory Evidence of ID	ID Number
❑ Acknowledgment	❑ Driver's License ❑ ID Card	
		Date Issued
❑ Oath/Affirmation	❑ Credible Witness ❑ Passport	
		Expiration Date
❑ Jurat	❑ Known Personally	
		Issuer
❑ Other_____	❑ Other: _____	

Printed Name of Witness		Signature
Address		Phone No.
		Email
Notes/Comments		Record No.

Printed Name of Signer		Signature	
Address		Phone No.	
		Email	

Date Notarized	Time	Am	Fee Charged	Travel Fee
		Pm		

Service	Satisfactory Evidence of ID	ID Number
❑ Acknowledgment	❑ Driver's License ❑ ID Card	
		Date Issued
❑ Oath/Affirmation	❑ Credible Witness ❑ Passport	
		Expiration Date
❑ Jurat	❑ Known Personally	
		Issuer
❑ Other_____	❑ Other: _____	

Printed Name of Witness		Signature
Address		Phone No.
		Email
Notes/Comments		Record No.

Printed Name of Signer		Signature	
Address		Phone No.	
		Email	

Date Notarized	Time	Am Pm	Fee Charged	Travel Fee

Service	Satisfactory Evidence of ID		ID Number
❑ Acknowledgment	❑ Driver's License	❑ ID Card	Date Issued
❑ Oath/Affirmation	❑ Credible Witness	❑ Passport	Expiration Date
❑ Jurat	❑ Known Personally		Issuer
❑ Other_____	❑ Other: _____		

Printed Name of Witness	Signature
Address	Phone No.
	Email
Notes/Comments	Record No.

Printed Name of Signer		Signature	
Address		Phone No.	
		Email	

Date Notarized	Time	Am Pm	Fee Charged	Travel Fee

Service	Satisfactory Evidence of ID		ID Number
❑ Acknowledgment	❑ Driver's License	❑ ID Card	Date Issued
❑ Oath/Affirmation	❑ Credible Witness	❑ Passport	Expiration Date
❑ Jurat	❑ Known Personally		Issuer
❑ Other_____	❑ Other: _____		

Printed Name of Witness	Signature
Address	Phone No.
	Email
Notes/Comments	Record No.

Printed Name of Signer		Signature	
Address		Phone No.	
		Email	

Date Notarized	Time	Am	Fee Charged	Travel Fee
		Pm		

Service	Satisfactory Evidence of ID		ID Number
❑ Acknowledgment	❑ Driver's License	❑ ID Card	
			Date Issued
❑ Oath/Affirmation	❑ Credible Witness	❑ Passport	Expiration Date
❑ Jurat	❑ Known Personally		Issuer
❑ Other_____	❑ Other: _____		

Printed Name of Witness	Signature
Address	Phone No.
	Email
Notes/Comments	Record No.

Printed Name of Signer		Signature	
Address		Phone No.	
		Email	

Date Notarized	Time	Am	Fee Charged	Travel Fee
		Pm		

Service	Satisfactory Evidence of ID		ID Number
❑ Acknowledgment	❑ Driver's License	❑ ID Card	
			Date Issued
❑ Oath/Affirmation	❑ Credible Witness	❑ Passport	Expiration Date
❑ Jurat	❑ Known Personally		Issuer
❑ Other_____	❑ Other: _____		

Printed Name of Witness	Signature
Address	Phone No.
	Email
Notes/Comments	Record No.

Printed Name of Signer		Signature	

Address	Phone No.	
	Email	

Date Notarized	Time	Am	Fee Charged	Travel Fee
		Pm		

Service	Satisfactory Evidence of ID		ID Number
❑ Acknowledgment	❑ Driver's License	❑ ID Card	Date Issued
❑ Oath/Affirmation	❑ Credible Witness	❑ Passport	Expiration Date
❑ Jurat	❑ Known Personally		Issuer
❑ Other_____	❑ Other: _____		

Printed Name of Witness		Signature
Address	Phone No.	
	Email	
Notes/Comments	Record No.	

Printed Name of Signer		Signature	

Address	Phone No.	
	Email	

Date Notarized	Time	Am	Fee Charged	Travel Fee
		Pm		

Service	Satisfactory Evidence of ID		ID Number
❑ Acknowledgment	❑ Driver's License	❑ ID Card	Date Issued
❑ Oath/Affirmation	❑ Credible Witness	❑ Passport	Expiration Date
❑ Jurat	❑ Known Personally		Issuer
❑ Other_____	❑ Other: _____		

Printed Name of Witness		Signature
Address	Phone No.	
	Email	
Notes/Comments	Record No.	

Printed Name of Signer		Signature	
Address		Phone No.	
		Email	

Date Notarized	Time	Am Pm	Fee Charged	Travel Fee

Service	Satisfactory Evidence of ID		ID Number
❑ Acknowledgment	❑ Driver's License	❑ ID Card	Date Issued
❑ Oath/Affirmation	❑ Credible Witness	❑ Passport	Expiration Date
❑ Jurat	❑ Known Personally		Issuer
❑ Other_____	❑ Other: _____		

Printed Name of Witness	Signature
Address	Phone No.
	Email
Notes/Comments	Record No.

Printed Name of Signer		Signature	
Address		Phone No.	
		Email	

Date Notarized	Time	Am Pm	Fee Charged	Travel Fee

Service	Satisfactory Evidence of ID		ID Number
❑ Acknowledgment	❑ Driver's License	❑ ID Card	Date Issued
❑ Oath/Affirmation	❑ Credible Witness	❑ Passport	Expiration Date
❑ Jurat	❑ Known Personally		Issuer
❑ Other_____	❑ Other: _____		

Printed Name of Witness	Signature
Address	Phone No.
	Email
Notes/Comments	Record No.

Printed Name of Signer			Signature	
Address			Phone No.	
			Email	

Date Notarized	Time	Am	Fee Charged	Travel Fee
		Pm		

Service	Satisfactory Evidence of ID		ID Number
❑ Acknowledgment	❑ Driver's License	❑ ID Card	
			Date Issued
❑ Oath/Affirmation	❑ Credible Witness	❑ Passport	
			Expiration Date
❑ Jurat	❑ Known Personally		
			Issuer
❑ Other_____	❑ Other: _____		

Printed Name of Witness	Signature
Address	Phone No.
	Email
Notes/Comments	Record No.

Printed Name of Signer			Signature	
Address			Phone No.	
			Email	

Date Notarized	Time	Am	Fee Charged	Travel Fee
		Pm		

Service	Satisfactory Evidence of ID		ID Number
❑ Acknowledgment	❑ Driver's License	❑ ID Card	
			Date Issued
❑ Oath/Affirmation	❑ Credible Witness	❑ Passport	
			Expiration Date
❑ Jurat	❑ Known Personally		
			Issuer
❑ Other_____	❑ Other: _____		

Printed Name of Witness	Signature
Address	Phone No.
	Email
Notes/Comments	Record No.

Printed Name of Signer		Signature	

Address		Phone No.	
		Email	

Date Notarized	Time	Am	Fee Charged	Travel Fee
		Pm		

Service	Satisfactory Evidence of ID		ID Number
❑ Acknowledgment	❑ Driver's License	❑ ID Card	
			Date Issued
❑ Oath/Affirmation	❑ Credible Witness	❑ Passport	
			Expiration Date
❑ Jurat	❑ Known Personally		
			Issuer
❑ Other_____	❑ Other: _____		

Printed Name of Witness	Signature
Address	Phone No.
	Email
Notes/Comments	Record No.

Printed Name of Signer		Signature	

Address		Phone No.	
		Email	

Date Notarized	Time	Am	Fee Charged	Travel Fee
		Pm		

Service	Satisfactory Evidence of ID		ID Number
❑ Acknowledgment	❑ Driver's License	❑ ID Card	
			Date Issued
❑ Oath/Affirmation	❑ Credible Witness	❑ Passport	
			Expiration Date
❑ Jurat	❑ Known Personally		
			Issuer
❑ Other_____	❑ Other: _____		

Printed Name of Witness	Signature
Address	Phone No.
	Email
Notes/Comments	Record No.

Printed Name of Signer		Signature	
Address		Phone No.	
		Email	

Date Notarized	Time	Am Pm	Fee Charged	Travel Fee

Service	Satisfactory Evidence of ID		ID Number
❑ Acknowledgment	❑ Driver's License	❑ ID Card	
			Date Issued
❑ Oath/Affirmation	❑ Credible Witness	❑ Passport	Expiration Date
❑ Jurat	❑ Known Personally		Issuer
❑ Other_____	❑ Other: _____		

Printed Name of Witness	Signature
Address	Phone No.
	Email
Notes/Comments	Record No.

Printed Name of Signer		Signature	
Address		Phone No.	
		Email	

Date Notarized	Time	Am Pm	Fee Charged	Travel Fee

Service	Satisfactory Evidence of ID		ID Number
❑ Acknowledgment	❑ Driver's License	❑ ID Card	
			Date Issued
❑ Oath/Affirmation	❑ Credible Witness	❑ Passport	Expiration Date
❑ Jurat	❑ Known Personally		Issuer
❑ Other_____	❑ Other: _____		

Printed Name of Witness	Signature
Address	Phone No.
	Email
Notes/Comments	Record No.

Printed Name of Signer		Signature	
Address		Phone No.	
		Email	

Date Notarized	Time	Am Pm	Fee Charged	Travel Fee

Service	Satisfactory Evidence of ID		ID Number
❑ Acknowledgment	❑ Driver's License	❑ ID Card	Date Issued
❑ Oath/Affirmation	❑ Credible Witness	❑ Passport	Expiration Date
❑ Jurat	❑ Known Personally		Issuer
❑ Other_____	❑ Other: _____		

Printed Name of Witness	Signature
Address	Phone No.
	Email
Notes/Comments	Record No.

Printed Name of Signer		Signature	
Address		Phone No.	
		Email	

Date Notarized	Time	Am Pm	Fee Charged	Travel Fee

Service	Satisfactory Evidence of ID		ID Number
❑ Acknowledgment	❑ Driver's License	❑ ID Card	Date Issued
❑ Oath/Affirmation	❑ Credible Witness	❑ Passport	Expiration Date
❑ Jurat	❑ Known Personally		Issuer
❑ Other_____	❑ Other: _____		

Printed Name of Witness	Signature
Address	Phone No.
	Email
Notes/Comments	Record No.

Printed Name of Signer		Signature	
Address		Phone No.	
		Email	

Date Notarized	Time	Am	Fee Charged	Travel Fee
		Pm		

Service	Satisfactory Evidence of ID		ID Number
❑ Acknowledgment	❑ Driver's License	❑ ID Card	
			Date Issued
❑ Oath/Affirmation	❑ Credible Witness	❑ Passport	
			Expiration Date
❑ Jurat	❑ Known Personally		
			Issuer
❑ Other_____	❑ Other: _____		

Printed Name of Witness	Signature
Address	Phone No.
	Email
Notes/Comments	Record No.

Printed Name of Signer		Signature	
Address		Phone No.	
		Email	

Date Notarized	Time	Am	Fee Charged	Travel Fee
		Pm		

Service	Satisfactory Evidence of ID		ID Number
❑ Acknowledgment	❑ Driver's License	❑ ID Card	
			Date Issued
❑ Oath/Affirmation	❑ Credible Witness	❑ Passport	
			Expiration Date
❑ Jurat	❑ Known Personally		
			Issuer
❑ Other_____	❑ Other: _____		

Printed Name of Witness	Signature
Address	Phone No.
	Email
Notes/Comments	Record No.

Printed Name of Signer		Signature	
Address		Phone No.	
		Email	

Date Notarized	Time	Am	Fee Charged	Travel Fee
		Pm		

Service	Satisfactory Evidence of ID	ID Number
❑ Acknowledgment	❑ Driver's License ❑ ID Card	Date Issued
❑ Oath/Affirmation	❑ Credible Witness ❑ Passport	Expiration Date
❑ Jurat	❑ Known Personally	Issuer
❑ Other_____	❑ Other: _____	

Printed Name of Witness		Signature
Address		Phone No.
		Email
Notes/Comments		Record No.

Printed Name of Signer		Signature	
Address		Phone No.	
		Email	

Date Notarized	Time	Am	Fee Charged	Travel Fee
		Pm		

Service	Satisfactory Evidence of ID	ID Number
❑ Acknowledgment	❑ Driver's License ❑ ID Card	Date Issued
❑ Oath/Affirmation	❑ Credible Witness ❑ Passport	Expiration Date
❑ Jurat	❑ Known Personally	Issuer
❑ Other_____	❑ Other: _____	

Printed Name of Witness		Signature
Address		Phone No.
		Email
Notes/Comments		Record No.

Printed Name of Signer		Signature	
Address		Phone No.	
		Email	

Date Notarized	Time	Am	Fee Charged	Travel Fee
		Pm		

Service	Satisfactory Evidence of ID		ID Number
❑ Acknowledgment	❑ Driver's License	❑ ID Card	
			Date Issued
❑ Oath/Affirmation	❑ Credible Witness	❑ Passport	
			Expiration Date
❑ Jurat	❑ Known Personally		
			Issuer
❑ Other_____	❑ Other: _____		

Printed Name of Witness		Signature
Address		Phone No.
		Email
Notes/Comments		Record No.

Printed Name of Signer		Signature	
Address		Phone No.	
		Email	

Date Notarized	Time	Am	Fee Charged	Travel Fee
		Pm		

Service	Satisfactory Evidence of ID		ID Number
❑ Acknowledgment	❑ Driver's License	❑ ID Card	
			Date Issued
❑ Oath/Affirmation	❑ Credible Witness	❑ Passport	
			Expiration Date
❑ Jurat	❑ Known Personally		
			Issuer
❑ Other_____	❑ Other: _____		

Printed Name of Witness		Signature
Address		Phone No.
		Email
Notes/Comments		Record No.

Printed Name of Signer		Signature	
Address		Phone No.	
		Email	

Date Notarized	Time	Am	Fee Charged	Travel Fee
		Pm		

Service	Satisfactory Evidence of ID	ID Number
❏ Acknowledgment	❏ Driver's License ❏ ID Card	Date Issued
❏ Oath/Affirmation	❏ Credible Witness ❏ Passport	Expiration Date
❏ Jurat	❏ Known Personally	Issuer
❏ Other_____	❏ Other: _____	

Printed Name of Witness		Signature
Address		Phone No.
		Email
Notes/Comments		Record No.

Printed Name of Signer		Signature	
Address		Phone No.	
		Email	

Date Notarized	Time	Am	Fee Charged	Travel Fee
		Pm		

Service	Satisfactory Evidence of ID	ID Number
❏ Acknowledgment	❏ Driver's License ❏ ID Card	Date Issued
❏ Oath/Affirmation	❏ Credible Witness ❏ Passport	Expiration Date
❏ Jurat	❏ Known Personally	Issuer
❏ Other_____	❏ Other: _____	

Printed Name of Witness		Signature
Address		Phone No.
		Email
Notes/Comments		Record No.

Printed Name of Signer		Signature	
Address		Phone No.	
		Email	

Date Notarized	Time	Am	Fee Charged	Travel Fee
		Pm		

Service	Satisfactory Evidence of ID		ID Number
❑ Acknowledgment	❑ Driver's License	❑ ID Card	Date Issued
❑ Oath/Affirmation	❑ Credible Witness	❑ Passport	Expiration Date
❑ Jurat	❑ Known Personally		Issuer
❑ Other_____	❑ Other: _____		

Printed Name of Witness		Signature	
Address		Phone No.	
		Email	
Notes/Comments		Record No.	

Printed Name of Signer		Signature	
Address		Phone No.	
		Email	

Date Notarized	Time	Am	Fee Charged	Travel Fee
		Pm		

Service	Satisfactory Evidence of ID		ID Number
❑ Acknowledgment	❑ Driver's License	❑ ID Card	Date Issued
❑ Oath/Affirmation	❑ Credible Witness	❑ Passport	Expiration Date
❑ Jurat	❑ Known Personally		Issuer
❑ Other_____	❑ Other: _____		

Printed Name of Witness		Signature	
Address		Phone No.	
		Email	
Notes/Comments		Record No.	

Printed Name of Signer		Signature	
Address		**Phone No.**	
		Email	

Date Notarized	Time	Am Pm	Fee Charged	Travel Fee

Service	Satisfactory Evidence of ID		ID Number
❑ Acknowledgment	❑ Driver's License	❑ ID Card	Date Issued
❑ Oath/Affirmation	❑ Credible Witness	❑ Passport	Expiration Date
❑ Jurat	❑ Known Personally		Issuer
❑ Other_____	❑ Other: _____		

Printed Name of Witness	Signature
Address	**Phone No.**
	Email
Notes/Comments	**Record No.**

Printed Name of Signer		Signature	
Address		**Phone No.**	
		Email	

Date Notarized	Time	Am Pm	Fee Charged	Travel Fee

Service	Satisfactory Evidence of ID		ID Number
❑ Acknowledgment	❑ Driver's License	❑ ID Card	Date Issued
❑ Oath/Affirmation	❑ Credible Witness	❑ Passport	Expiration Date
❑ Jurat	❑ Known Personally		Issuer
❑ Other_____	❑ Other: _____		

Printed Name of Witness	Signature
Address	**Phone No.**
	Email
Notes/Comments	**Record No.**

Printed Name of Signer		Signature	
Address		Phone No.	
		Email	

Date Notarized	Time	Am	Fee Charged	Travel Fee
		Pm		

Service	Satisfactory Evidence of ID		ID Number
❑ Acknowledgment	❑ Driver's License	❑ ID Card	Date Issued
❑ Oath/Affirmation	❑ Credible Witness	❑ Passport	Expiration Date
❑ Jurat	❑ Known Personally		Issuer
❑ Other_____	❑ Other: _____		

Printed Name of Witness	Signature
Address	Phone No.
	Email
Notes/Comments	Record No.

Printed Name of Signer		Signature	
Address		Phone No.	
		Email	

Date Notarized	Time	Am	Fee Charged	Travel Fee
		Pm		

Service	Satisfactory Evidence of ID		ID Number
❑ Acknowledgment	❑ Driver's License	❑ ID Card	Date Issued
❑ Oath/Affirmation	❑ Credible Witness	❑ Passport	Expiration Date
❑ Jurat	❑ Known Personally		Issuer
❑ Other_____	❑ Other: _____		

Printed Name of Witness	Signature
Address	Phone No.
	Email
Notes/Comments	Record No.

Printed Name of Signer			Signature	
Address		Phone No.		
		Email		
Date Notarized	Time	Am / Pm	Fee Charged	Travel Fee

Service	Satisfactory Evidence of ID		ID Number
❑ Acknowledgment	❑ Driver's License	❑ ID Card	Date Issued
❑ Oath/Affirmation	❑ Credible Witness	❑ Passport	Expiration Date
❑ Jurat	❑ Known Personally		Issuer
❑ Other_____	❑ Other: _____		

Printed Name of Witness	Signature
Address	Phone No.
	Email
Notes/Comments	Record No.

Printed Name of Signer			Signature	
Address		Phone No.		
		Email		
Date Notarized	Time	Am / Pm	Fee Charged	Travel Fee

Service	Satisfactory Evidence of ID		ID Number
❑ Acknowledgment	❑ Driver's License	❑ ID Card	Date Issued
❑ Oath/Affirmation	❑ Credible Witness	❑ Passport	Expiration Date
❑ Jurat	❑ Known Personally		Issuer
❑ Other_____	❑ Other: _____		

Printed Name of Witness	Signature
Address	Phone No.
	Email
Notes/Comments	Record No.

Printed Name of Signer		Signature	
Address		Phone No.	
		Email	

Date Notarized	Time	Am	Fee Charged	Travel Fee
		Pm		

Service	Satisfactory Evidence of ID		ID Number
❑ Acknowledgment	❑ Driver's License	❑ ID Card	Date Issued
❑ Oath/Affirmation	❑ Credible Witness	❑ Passport	Expiration Date
❑ Jurat	❑ Known Personally		Issuer
❑ Other_____	❑ Other: _____		

Printed Name of Witness	Signature
Address	Phone No.
	Email
Notes/Comments	Record No.

Printed Name of Signer		Signature	
Address		Phone No.	
		Email	

Date Notarized	Time	Am	Fee Charged	Travel Fee
		Pm		

Service	Satisfactory Evidence of ID		ID Number
❑ Acknowledgment	❑ Driver's License	❑ ID Card	Date Issued
❑ Oath/Affirmation	❑ Credible Witness	❑ Passport	Expiration Date
❑ Jurat	❑ Known Personally		Issuer
❑ Other_____	❑ Other: _____		

Printed Name of Witness	Signature
Address	Phone No.
	Email
Notes/Comments	Record No.

Printed Name of Signer		Signature	
Address		Phone No.	
		Email	

Date Notarized	Time	Am	Fee Charged	Travel Fee
		Pm		

Service	Satisfactory Evidence of ID		ID Number
❑ Acknowledgment	❑ Driver's License	❑ ID Card	
			Date Issued
❑ Oath/Affirmation	❑ Credible Witness	❑ Passport	
			Expiration Date
❑ Jurat	❑ Known Personally		
			Issuer
❑ Other_____	❑ Other: _____		

Printed Name of Witness	Signature
Address	Phone No.
	Email
Notes/Comments	Record No.

Printed Name of Signer		Signature	
Address		Phone No.	
		Email	

Date Notarized	Time	Am	Fee Charged	Travel Fee
		Pm		

Service	Satisfactory Evidence of ID		ID Number
❑ Acknowledgment	❑ Driver's License	❑ ID Card	
			Date Issued
❑ Oath/Affirmation	❑ Credible Witness	❑ Passport	
			Expiration Date
❑ Jurat	❑ Known Personally		
			Issuer
❑ Other_____	❑ Other: _____		

Printed Name of Witness	Signature
Address	Phone No.
	Email
Notes/Comments	Record No.

Printed Name of Signer		Signature	
Address		Phone No.	
		Email	

Date Notarized	Time	Am	Fee Charged	Travel Fee
		Pm		

Service	Satisfactory Evidence of ID		ID Number
☐ Acknowledgment	☐ Driver's License	☐ ID Card	
			Date Issued
☐ Oath/Affirmation	☐ Credible Witness	☐ Passport	
			Expiration Date
☐ Jurat	☐ Known Personally		
			Issuer
☐ Other_____	☐ Other: _____		

Printed Name of Witness	Signature
Address	Phone No.
	Email
Notes/Comments	Record No.

Printed Name of Signer		Signature	
Address		Phone No.	
		Email	

Date Notarized	Time	Am	Fee Charged	Travel Fee
		Pm		

Service	Satisfactory Evidence of ID		ID Number
☐ Acknowledgment	☐ Driver's License	☐ ID Card	
			Date Issued
☐ Oath/Affirmation	☐ Credible Witness	☐ Passport	
			Expiration Date
☐ Jurat	☐ Known Personally		
			Issuer
☐ Other_____	☐ Other: _____		

Printed Name of Witness	Signature
Address	Phone No.
	Email
Notes/Comments	Record No.

Printed Name of Signer		Signature	
Address		Phone No.	
		Email	

Date Notarized	Time	Am Pm	Fee Charged	Travel Fee

Service	Satisfactory Evidence of ID	ID Number
❑ Acknowledgment	❑ Driver's License ❑ ID Card	
		Date Issued
❑ Oath/Affirmation	❑ Credible Witness ❑ Passport	
		Expiration Date
❑ Jurat	❑ Known Personally	
		Issuer
❑ Other_____	❑ Other: _____	

Printed Name of Witness		Signature	
Address		Phone No.	
		Email	
Notes/Comments		Record No.	

Printed Name of Signer		Signature	
Address		Phone No.	
		Email	

Date Notarized	Time	Am Pm	Fee Charged	Travel Fee

Service	Satisfactory Evidence of ID	ID Number
❑ Acknowledgment	❑ Driver's License ❑ ID Card	
		Date Issued
❑ Oath/Affirmation	❑ Credible Witness ❑ Passport	
		Expiration Date
❑ Jurat	❑ Known Personally	
		Issuer
❑ Other_____	❑ Other: _____	

Printed Name of Witness		Signature	
Address		Phone No.	
		Email	
Notes/Comments		Record No.	

Printed Name of Signer		Signature	
Address		Phone No.	
		Email	

Date Notarized	Time	Am	Fee Charged	Travel Fee
		Pm		

Service	Satisfactory Evidence of ID		ID Number
❑ Acknowledgment	❑ Driver's License	❑ ID Card	
			Date Issued
❑ Oath/Affirmation	❑ Credible Witness	❑ Passport	
			Expiration Date
❑ Jurat	❑ Known Personally		
			Issuer
❑ Other_____	❑ Other: _____		

Printed Name of Witness	Signature
Address	Phone No.
	Email
Notes/Comments	Record No.

Printed Name of Signer		Signature	
Address		Phone No.	
		Email	

Date Notarized	Time	Am	Fee Charged	Travel Fee
		Pm		

Service	Satisfactory Evidence of ID		ID Number
❑ Acknowledgment	❑ Driver's License	❑ ID Card	
			Date Issued
❑ Oath/Affirmation	❑ Credible Witness	❑ Passport	
			Expiration Date
❑ Jurat	❑ Known Personally		
			Issuer
❑ Other_____	❑ Other: _____		

Printed Name of Witness	Signature
Address	Phone No.
	Email
Notes/Comments	Record No.

Printed Name of Signer		Signature	
Address		Phone No.	
		Email	

Date Notarized	Time	Am	Fee Charged	Travel Fee
		Pm		

Service	Satisfactory Evidence of ID		ID Number
❏ Acknowledgment	❏ Driver's License	❏ ID Card	Date Issued
❏ Oath/Affirmation	❏ Credible Witness	❏ Passport	Expiration Date
❏ Jurat	❏ Known Personally		Issuer
❏ Other_____	❏ Other: _____		

Printed Name of Witness	Signature
Address	Phone No.
	Email
Notes/Comments	Record No.

Printed Name of Signer		Signature	
Address		Phone No.	
		Email	

Date Notarized	Time	Am	Fee Charged	Travel Fee
		Pm		

Service	Satisfactory Evidence of ID		ID Number
❏ Acknowledgment	❏ Driver's License	❏ ID Card	Date Issued
❏ Oath/Affirmation	❏ Credible Witness	❏ Passport	Expiration Date
❏ Jurat	❏ Known Personally		Issuer
❏ Other_____	❏ Other: _____		

Printed Name of Witness	Signature
Address	Phone No.
	Email
Notes/Comments	Record No.

Printed Name of Signer		Signature	

Address		Phone No.	
		Email	

Date Notarized	Time	Am	Fee Charged	Travel Fee
		Pm		

Service	Satisfactory Evidence of ID		ID Number
❑ Acknowledgment	❑ Driver's License	❑ ID Card	
			Date Issued
❑ Oath/Affirmation	❑ Credible Witness	❑ Passport	
			Expiration Date
❑ Jurat	❑ Known Personally		
			Issuer
❑ Other_____	❑ Other: _____		

Printed Name of Witness	Signature

Address	Phone No.
	Email

Notes/Comments	Record No.

Printed Name of Signer		Signature	

Address		Phone No.	
		Email	

Date Notarized	Time	Am	Fee Charged	Travel Fee
		Pm		

Service	Satisfactory Evidence of ID		ID Number
❑ Acknowledgment	❑ Driver's License	❑ ID Card	
			Date Issued
❑ Oath/Affirmation	❑ Credible Witness	❑ Passport	
			Expiration Date
❑ Jurat	❑ Known Personally		
			Issuer
❑ Other_____	❑ Other: _____		

Printed Name of Witness	Signature

Address	Phone No.
	Email

Notes/Comments	Record No.

Printed Name of Signer		Signature	
Address		Phone No.	
		Email	

Date Notarized	Time	Am	Fee Charged	Travel Fee
		Pm		

Service	Satisfactory Evidence of ID		ID Number
❑ Acknowledgment	❑ Driver's License	❑ ID Card	Date Issued
❑ Oath/Affirmation	❑ Credible Witness	❑ Passport	Expiration Date
❑ Jurat	❑ Known Personally		Issuer
❑ Other_____	❑ Other: _____		

Printed Name of Witness	Signature
Address	Phone No.
	Email
Notes/Comments	Record No.

Printed Name of Signer		Signature	
Address		Phone No.	
		Email	

Date Notarized	Time	Am	Fee Charged	Travel Fee
		Pm		

Service	Satisfactory Evidence of ID		ID Number
❑ Acknowledgment	❑ Driver's License	❑ ID Card	Date Issued
❑ Oath/Affirmation	❑ Credible Witness	❑ Passport	Expiration Date
❑ Jurat	❑ Known Personally		Issuer
❑ Other_____	❑ Other: _____		

Printed Name of Witness	Signature
Address	Phone No.
	Email
Notes/Comments	Record No.

Printed Name of Signer			Signature	
Address			Phone No.	
			Email	

Date Notarized	Time	Am / Pm	Fee Charged	Travel Fee

Service	Satisfactory Evidence of ID		ID Number
❑ Acknowledgment	❑ Driver's License	❑ ID Card	Date Issued
❑ Oath/Affirmation	❑ Credible Witness	❑ Passport	Expiration Date
❑ Jurat	❑ Known Personally		Issuer
❑ Other_____	❑ Other: _____		

Printed Name of Witness	Signature
Address	Phone No.
	Email
Notes/Comments	Record No.

Printed Name of Signer			Signature	
Address			Phone No.	
			Email	

Date Notarized	Time	Am / Pm	Fee Charged	Travel Fee

Service	Satisfactory Evidence of ID		ID Number
❑ Acknowledgment	❑ Driver's License	❑ ID Card	Date Issued
❑ Oath/Affirmation	❑ Credible Witness	❑ Passport	Expiration Date
❑ Jurat	❑ Known Personally		Issuer
❑ Other_____	❑ Other: _____		

Printed Name of Witness	Signature
Address	Phone No.
	Email
Notes/Comments	Record No.

Printed Name of Signer		Signature	
Address		Phone No.	
		Email	

Date Notarized	Time	Am Pm	Fee Charged	Travel Fee

Service	Satisfactory Evidence of ID		ID Number
❏ Acknowledgment	❏ Driver's License	❏ ID Card	Date Issued
❏ Oath/Affirmation	❏ Credible Witness	❏ Passport	Expiration Date
❏ Jurat	❏ Known Personally		Issuer
❏ Other_____	❏ Other: _____		

Printed Name of Witness	Signature
Address	Phone No.
	Email
Notes/Comments	Record No.

Printed Name of Signer		Signature	
Address		Phone No.	
		Email	

Date Notarized	Time	Am Pm	Fee Charged	Travel Fee

Service	Satisfactory Evidence of ID		ID Number
❏ Acknowledgment	❏ Driver's License	❏ ID Card	Date Issued
❏ Oath/Affirmation	❏ Credible Witness	❏ Passport	Expiration Date
❏ Jurat	❏ Known Personally		Issuer
❏ Other_____	❏ Other: _____		

Printed Name of Witness	Signature
Address	Phone No.
	Email
Notes/Comments	Record No.